Financing and Problems of Development Banking

PRAEGER SPECIAL STUDIES IN
INTERNATIONAL ECONOMICS AND DEVELOPMENT

Financing and Problems of Development Banking

Prepared for the
FUND FOR INTERNATIONAL
COOPERATIVE DEVELOPMENT

by J.T. Dock Houk

FREDERICK A. PRAEGER, Publishers
New York · Washington · London

The purpose of the Praeger Special Studies is to make specialized research monographs in U.S. and international economics and politics
available to the academic, business, and government communities. For
further information, write to the Special Projects Division, Frederick
A. Praeger, Publishers, 111 Fourth Avenue, New York, N.Y. 10003.

FREDERICK A. PRAEGER, PUBLISHERS
111 Fourth Avenue, New York, N.Y. 10003, U.S.A.
77-79 Charlotte Street, London W.1, England

Published in the United States of America in 1967
by Frederick A. Praeger, Inc., Publishers

Library of Congress Catalog Card Number: 66-26564

Printed in the United States of America

PREFACE

This study attempts to illuminate certain aspects of development banking, including a definition of the term, an analysis of the relationships between inflation and bank operation, and financing.

It is based on research done as a part of the Inter-American Cooperative Bank Development Program, which is designed to strengthen the cooperative finance system in Latin America by setting up an integrated system of development banks for cooperatives among the countries in Latin America where such assistance is appropriate. The study, which was financed under a contract between the Fund for International Cooperative Development and the Agency for International Development, was for general information purposes only and not to foster any particular cooperative finance system.

The Fund for International Cooperative Development is grateful to Mr. J. T. Dock Houk for the research and writing which he undertook for this study as a part of his work for the Inter-American Cooperative Bank Development Program. Mr. Houk had valuable assistance and advice from officials of the Inter-American Development Bank, International Finance Corporation, Massachusetts Institute of Technology, and the Agency for International Development as well as from colleagues in the Inter-American Cooperative Bank Development Program in the preparation of this study. To all of these agencies we extend our appreciation.

Hector Zayas-Chardon
Director

Inter-American Cooperative
Bank Development Program

CONTENTS

LIST OF TABLES

ABBREVIATIONS

AID	Agency for International Development
BID	Inter-American Development Bank referred to by Latin Americans as "El BID"
CABEI	Central American Bank for Economic Integration
CCCE	Caisse Centrale de Cooperation Economique
CDC	Commonwealth Development Corporation
CDC	Cyprus Development Corporation
CORFO	Corporación de Fomento de la Producción
IADB	Inter-American Development Bank
IBRD	International Bank for Reconstruction and Development
ICICI	Industrial Credit and Investment Corporation of India
IDA	International Development Association
IDB	Industrial Development Bank
IDB/T	Industrial Development Bank of Turkey
IFC	International Finance Corporation
IFICOOP	Chile Cooperative Finance Institute
IMDBI	Industrial Mining and Development Bank of Iran
IMF	International Monetary Fund
INCORA	Instituto Colombiano de Reforma Agraria

NESA	Near East South Asia
NIDB	Nigerian Industrial Development Bank
OAS	Organization of American States
PDC	Private Development Corporation of the Philippines
PICIC	Pakistan Industrial Credit and Investment Corporation

CHAPTER **1** TOWARD
A DEFINITION
OF DEVELOPMENT
BANKING

The rapid growth of an institution in the developing countries, known as a development bank or a development finance
company, has been observed with great interest by practitioners in the field of economic development. The Agency
for International Development reported in October of 1964
that during the period September, 1951 - June, 1964, it had
provided financial assistance in the form of grants or loans
of dollars or local currency in the amount of $1.3 billion to
106 separate intermediate credit institutions located in 48
countries.[1]

A recent series of issues of Business International[2] indicated that in Latin America alone there were 57 public,
private, and mixed development banks in 25 countries and
territories. The implicit but unstated definition of development banks used in the Business International compilation
was "an institution which provided either loans and/or equity
to industrial projects." Undoubtedly this list would have been
even longer if we had attempted to include financial institutions that relate to the development of agriculture, housing,
cooperatives, or of any other sector of a developing economy
which needs finances to grow.

A FUNCTIONAL APPROACH TO A DEFINITION
OF DEVELOPMENT BANKING

The World Bank, the Agency for International Development (and predecessors) and more recently the International
Finance Corporation and the Inter-American Development
Bank have been the pioneers in the initiating and strengthening of development banking. Because most of their lending
has been to banks which have re-lent for industrial projects,
there has been an increasing tendency to associate development banking only with industrial project financing.

1

It seems best, however, to approach the definition of development banking from a functional point of view: that is, to determine whether an institution is a development bank by observing the functions which it is performing or is designed to perform within a developing economy. We could say, therefore, that an institution would be classified as a development bank if it were designed to perform both banking and development functions.

Banking Function

The principal financial function that a development bank must perform is the provision of medium- and long-term capital to economic development projects. It is certainly not necessary that these projects be restricted to the field of industrial development, although history has shown that here is an area which a country determined to increase its per capita production must not overlook. However, projects which stimulate agricultural development or which relate to the development of a country's infrastructure or which stimulate the growth of certain institutions such as cooperatives, can, in specific instances, have as much or more impact on economic development.

Other financial functions of a development bank apply as much to industrial banking as to any other type of development banking and include the investment by the bank in the equity of a borrower, the guaranteeing of a loan by a third party to a borrower, the underwriting of attempts by a borrower to raise equity or debt and the service of providing broad financial contacts both within and outside of the developing country.

Development Function

A financing institution which restricts its activities only to the banking functions mentioned above should not be classified as a development bank. A development bank must, in addition to its banking function, attempt to relate to certain problems of, or bottlenecks to, development, the magnitude and importance of which may vary from country to country. Four typical problems are enumerated below, together with some indication of how a development bank might approach them.

Critical Shortage of Viable Projects

Few observers will disagree with the statement that the principal problem facing intermediate credit institutions, development banks, in the world today is a shortage of viable projects presented to the bank in a "bankable form" as applications for loans or opportunities for investment. For the lack of projects, among other things, many development banks have found that funds provided to them by international lending agencies have moved rather slowly and, because development banks have had to work carefully with applicants in order to help them build into their projects elements of viability, development banking has tended to be more expensive per dollar committed than it otherwise might be.

Development banks have attempted many different approaches to this problem. Banco do Nordeste in Brazil, for example, collaborated with AID, the Ford Foundation, and other financial institutions to bring a project team from UCLA, under the leadership of Professor Morris Asimow, which initially combined with a group from the University of Ceara. This combined team initiated feasibility studies on several industries, presented these studies to local townspeople and tradesmen, and catalyzed the formation of stock-owning corporations to take advantage of the industrial and agricultural development opportunities thus identified. The Nepal Industrial Development Corporation asked for, and received, an AID grant to support a team of experts to promote and develop industrial projects.

A development bank must be extremely careful in project development for two reasons: first, because project development is costly; and second, because the development bank may find itself in the awkward position of recommending a project to itself for financing. It is, indeed, this latter reason that has initiated a movement in Nepal to separate the Nepal Industrial Development Corporation from its technical assistance function.

The technique developed by the Banco do Nordeste in Brazil, that of participating in the cost of a project development team, seems to be an ideal method of combining an impact on the project shortage with the necessity of preserving the independence of the development bank to judge the project on its merits when it is presented to the bank for a loan.

Lack of Business Skills

The lack of business skills in a developing country is definitely related to Critical Shortage of Viable Projects above. One of the reasons for the shortage of viable projects being submitted to a development bank is the inability of prospective entrepreneurs to think through all aspects of a project before they submit it to the development bank for financing.

A development bank has two separate opportunities to assist in bolstering the business skills of its borrowers. The first is in the application stage, when bank personnel have an opportunity to work with the borrower. The second is in the implementation stage of a loan, when upon request, or when signs of trouble appear in the financial reports or are otherwise noticed by the bank, the bank is again in a position to assist the borrower. Bank assistance in either of these stages may be of two kinds: (1) It may provide this assistance from its own specialized resources, or (2) it may coordinate outside resources both within the country and from abroad to meet the needs of the borrower.

Obviously, providing this assistance from its own resources can be a very costly approach to the problem. Whether a development bank indeed staffs itself to provide this assistance will depend on many factors. Among them are: its own earnings or profitability, its feeling of responsibility toward the owners of the equity capital, the existence of other institutions within the country capable of performing this function, and the depth of the lack of business skills.

The contract team which has presently been assisting the Nepal Industrial Development Corporation to generate viable projects has found it necessary to give basic business education services, such as lectures and seminars in accounting techniques, business management practices, or marketing analysis to the management of existing or prospective borrowers. Other development banks have been successful in encouraging borrowers to enter upon joint ventures in which their partner, in addition to providing some financial assistance, would be experienced in the business and able to impart to the business the benefit of his experience.

Some of the documents supporting the recently formed

International Executive Service Corps have pointed out that this organization might be able to provide experts in various fields of business to development banks for precisely this purpose. These experts and their advice would be at the disposition of borrowers or prospective borrowers from the development bank.

Fostering a Capital Market

Developing countries which respect and value the positive incentive of profits as a stimulus to investment and which are trying to remove from the shoulders of entrepreneurs the fetters of state control, realize that they must have an impact on the development of a capital market. The concept of a capital market includes the complex of institutions in a country which affects the generation of savings and effects its transfer to those who will invest.

The complex of institutions referred to above includes the demanders of capital, such as corporations, partnerships, and single proprietors; institutions which supply capital and which generate capital in a form available to satisfy investment demand, such as banks, insurance companies, investment trusts, etc. and what may be called facilitating institutions, such as stock exchanges and institutions which perform the functions of underwriting, guaranteeing, insuring, etc.

Institutions, especially in a developing country, are not created in a vacuum. They are responses to, and in turn are molded by, the environment in which they arise. The complex of institutions, which forms a capital market, and their structure and operations are affected by many factors over which the development bank has no control, such as political instability, attitudes toward savings, especially in the light of price instability or political security, and the existing structure of business organization and its method of operation.

However, there is a great deal a development bank can do toward the stimulation and strengthening of a capital market, such as:

a. Issue, Promote, and Sell Its Own Equity Instruments or Debt Obligations

Using the leverage of low-interest, long-term debt

capital (quasi-equity) many development banks have
been able to coax domestic and foreign private and
institutional savings into investments in the financial
structure of the development bank itself. Nacional
Financiera of Mexico is an example of a development
bank which is experimenting with a technique of relating certain stock issues to a specific investment
portfolio. The development banks for cooperatives
in the United States have developed a technique for
retiring capital by setting aside a portion of interest
charged on loans, which, together with a stock purchase requirement for new borrowers, acts in a
manner to revolve the capital of the bank. This technique appears especially appropriate in a developing
country to introduce gradually to a broad sector of
people the idea of owning and trading equity.

b. Purchase and Sale of Debt or Equity from Its
Portfolio

Many development banks have experimented with
the technique of selling from their portfolio. Indeed,
with some development banks, such as the Pakistan
Industrial Development Corporation, the requirement
to divest itself of its equity holdings is often built into
the participation agreement.

A development bank which wishes to stimulate the
capital market in this manner is faced with a dilemma
of either sacrificing its earning capacity by selling a
strong portion of its equity portfolio or else weakening
the capital market and the incentive of investors to
participate by selling the weaker portion of its equity
portfolio. In its formative years, a development bank
would be wise to take every precaution to avoid placing
its own financial structure in jeopardy. It is much
more important, in its early years, that a development bank succeed as a financial institution than that
it stimulate, in this way, the capital market.

c. Underwriting-Guaranteeing

Many development banks stimulate the capital
market by offering their services as underwriters
or as guarantors. As underwriters, they would

presumably stimulate the sales of debt instruments.

A development bank would probably delay its entry into this highly specialized field until it has establish-ed itself as an institution which can lend wisely to bor-rowers who pay principal and interest promptly. The Industrial Finance Corporation of India, for example, was in business for seven years (from 1948 to 1956) before it began to experiment with underwriting or guaranteeing. By 1956, its position in the Indian financial structure was established, and the bank per-sonnel had gained considerable experience in the operation of a development bank.

d. Participations

Because of its contacts with financial institutions, both within the country and abroad, a development bank very often can put together, or can assist the borrower to put together, the entire financial struc-ture of the project, and in thus bringing a willing buy-er and a willing seller of money together, a develop-ment bank, in itself, is performing one of the essen-tial functions of a capital market.

e. Generation of Confidence

One of the most important things that a develop-ment bank can do to stimulate the growth and strength-ening of a capital market is to generate confidence in commercial transactions. Development banks in Puerto Rico and South Africa, for example, have only to affix their stamp of approval on a project before funds often sufficient to finance the project are forth-coming. Indeed, a development bank which has the confidence of local and foreign institutional and pri-vate individual investors often finds its financial assistance unnecessary.

The operations of a development bank are seen by many as a means of familiarizing the public in lesser developed countries with industrial securities and as a means of both creating and seasoning securities for later wider ownership. Thus, to the extent to which the development bank achieves these objectives, to that extent it becomes a safe bridge over which capital can be induced to flow from savers to investors.

Implementation of Development Plans

Most developing countries, given scarce resources and unlimited wants, have begun to apply the use of these resources to the achievement of specific development objectives, or to the breaking or releasing of critical bottlenecks to the development. But one of the deficiencies in present attempts at national planning has been the task both of implementing the plan and of maintaining a strong optimistic private sector. Although the government is the most likely and the most usual controller and director of resources, through the use of its fiscal, monetary, and direct control powers, a development bank, too, can and should attempt to coordinate its investment objectives with the achievement of certain sectorial goals of the country's development plan.

At the present time, a great deal of attention is being directed by developmental economists to the agricultural sector; consequently, industrial development banks and other specialized development banks, such as agricultural development banks, or development banks for cooperatives, can and should direct their attention to projects which stimulate, rationalize, or otherwise make more effective agricultural production.

WORLD BANK-IFC ASSISTANCE TO DEVELOPMENT BANKS

An attempt to define a development bank ought to consider the de facto criteria which the World Bank and the IFC have used in their assistance to indigenous development banking efforts. Mr. William Diamond, presently the director of the department in IFC concerned with development finance companies, said that, as early as 1957,[3] the World Bank's experience with development banks, since their initial loan to the Industrial Bank of Turkey in 1949, had been sufficient for them to establish a model of what such institutions should be like. Their criteria included the following elements:

a. Private ownership and management;

b. A financial support from both foreign and domestic sources;

   c. A substantial amount of government funds, borrowed
      at the lowest possible cost (quasi-equity);

   d. A board of directors that reflects the broad interest
      of the community and of sufficient prestige as to be
      able to withstand both government and private
      pressures;

   e. Able and experienced management;

   f. A willingness to help develop the capital market; and

   g. A willingness, in addition to financial assistance, to
      provide or catalyze the provision of certain technical
      and managerial assistance as required.

This model has served for the development of many successful development banks, among them: the Industrial
Credit and Investment Corporation of India; the Pakistan Industrial Credit and Investment Corporation; and the Development Finance Corporation of Ceylon. With certain minor exceptions, the Industrial, Mining and Development Bank of
Iran, the Industrial Development Bank of Turkey, and several
other banks have also been set up on this model.

A more recent policy statement[4] of the IFC served to
underline many of the above points and to state again that the
purpose for which the development bank should be organized
would be to promote industrial and other development on
business principles, related to the sound economic growth of
the country.

Although the record to date indicates that the World Bank
family has imposed on itself the limitations of only investing
in private industrial banks, there appears to be no policy
reason why the World Bank and the IFC could not branch out
into other types of private development banking. The World
Bank has not lent to public development banks as a matter of
policy. IFC does not invest in them both as a matter of policy and because its Articles of Agreement specify that it may
invest only in private enterprise.

FOOTNOTE ON DEVELOPMENT BANKS FOR COOPERATIVES

An effort of recent origin is under way in Latin America

to explore the feasibility of setting up privately owned development banks for cooperatives. At the present time, there are three banks for cooperatives in operation: one in Ecuador, Banco de Cooperativas del Ecuador; the second one in Argentina, Banco Cooperativo Agrario Argentino; and the third in Chile, Instituto de Financiamiento Cooperativo. In addition, there are at present cooperative banks being organized in Colombia and the Dominican Republic, with technical assistance provided by the Agency for International Development, through a contract with the Fund for International Cooperative Development.

The program envisions that the banks for cooperatives will be woven into an integrated financing system by the setting up of an inter-American finance institution, which would be able to tap for relending to these banks sources of funds presently unavailable to them and, in addition, would provide operational guidelines and technical assistance.

This program appears to have certain special advantages that those concerned with development banking might find interesting. Probably most important is the potential that these institutions appear to have for a grass-roots popular impact. These banks are owned by cooperatives who have many thousands of members. The enthusiasm of a people for institutions which are truly their own and which are organized to serve their own financial requirements has been noted in the past and is expected to increase over the next few years.

Another advantage of development banks for cooperatives is that, although they are designed to serve the broad range of cooperatives, they tend to focus, as they have in the United States, on agricultural development, serving the farmer from production through processing to the ultimate consumer. Many of the participants at a conference held in AID on the development of national markets in Latin America, October 16-17, 1964, paid tribute to the contribution of cooperatives to the rationalization of production and marketing of agricultural products in the United States, and in addition to the potential of cooperatives to perform this same service in Latin America.

An advantage of a development bank for cooperatives as compared with banks which lend for infrastructural projects or even banks which lend for industrial development is that it

is likely to be less inflationary in its operation. A cooperative bank, especially one oriented toward farm production
credit, can and does focus on loans which have a very short
gestation period. This suggests that, even if a cooperative
bank were using funds which were potentially inflationary,
there would soon develop, from the use of the loan, product
sufficient to repay it. Similarly, many cooperative bank
loans would be oriented toward the rationalization of marketing systems and would, therefore, also tend to have a de-
flationary impact.

DEVELOPMENT BANKING IN PERSPECTIVE

It is only useful to define something if by this definition
we can form a clearer picture of what we are discussing. We
have here defined development banking to include all financial
institutions which have both financial and development functions. For some purposes, however, such as the development of detailed operational guidelines and specific organiza-
tional structures, it will be useful further to subdivide the
field into subcategories such as industrial development banking, agricultural development banking, small industry development corporations, development banks for cooperatives,
and the like.

For many other purposes, however, such as the dissem-
ination of information about sources and costs of funds, for
focusing on problems related to the form and method of technical assistance, for analysis of problems related to governmental fiscal and monetary policy, for analysis of the impact
of goals and objectives of development plans, and for the
formation of general guidelines relating to the structure and
organization of development banks, it may be useful to ad-
here to, and maintain, a larger view.

A country which seeks to achieve economic progress
over a broad range of economic and social development objectives will find it useful to have maximum coordination
among its institutions, especially in the financial market.
Experience gained in industrial development banking can be
extremely useful for practitioners in other types of development banks. Indeed, many development banks need experience in more than one field of development banking right
within their own four walls. For example, the Somali Republic now has a development bank, which, in view of the

serious need in that country for agricultural progress, and also in view of the shortage of personnel, will make loans for both industrial and agricultural projects. BCAIF in Lebanon has responsibilities in both the agricultural and industrial fields.

At present, there are certain national and international organizations which are attempting to forge formal structural ties to the field of development banking. There exists the possibility that these structural ties will be limited to industrial development banking. The Development Banking Loan Offices now located in one of the Regional Bureaus of AID, and now proposed for other AID Capital Development Offices, and the development banking focus presently existing in AID/ DFPE, in the Inter-American Development Bank and in the International Finance Corporation, can be of immeasurable value in developing broad guidelines for recommending patterns of development financing, in distilling techniques of organization and operation of development banks, and in sharpening the usefulness of development banks as tools of economic growth.

Institutional status is also valuable in the competition to obtain funds. To eliminate other types of development banking from the benefits of specialized structural ties seems to be a deterrent to all institutions involved. Country planners and government officials, when planning the institutional development of their country, will have to evaluate and choose from among a now rather loosely connected and heterogeneous assortment of development financing institutions.

Development banks are in transition. The beginnings of many institutions can be observed in the eclectic assortment of functions performed in an economy by a development bank, and time and development will more than likely see these emerge as separate institutions later on. For the present, however, it appears especially useful from many points of view to define development banking in such a way as to include the financing of economic development, through intermediate credit institutions, and the accompanying developmental function which these institutions can perform.

To define development banking to include a wider range of development financing institutions than just industrial project financing is only the first step. We then must see to it

that other types of development banks are woven into structures of national and international economic development institutions, so that they will receive the specialized analytical
and financial attention they deserve.

Notes to Chapter 1

1. See Unpublished Memorandum, dated October 8,
1964, from Seymour M. Peyser, Assistant Administrator for
Development Finance and Private Enterprise, Agency for
International Development, to the Administrator, Agency for
International Development, p. 1, Subject AID's Financial
Assistance to Intermediate Credit Institutions.

2. See Business International, August 28, 1964, p. 6;
September 4, 1964, p. 6; and September 18, 1964, p. 7.

3. William Diamond, "Some Comments on the
World Bank's Policies Concerning Experience With Development Banks, " unpublished paper, International Bank for
Reconstruction and Development, 1957.

4. International Finance Corporation, "Private Development Companies, " mimeographed: Washington, D.C.,
January 13, 1964.

2

DEVELOPMENT
BANKS
AND INFLATION

INFLATIONARY PRESSURES GENERATED
BY DEVELOPMENT

There has been quite a controversy in the literature about the relationship of inflation to economic growth. This controversy was sharpened but not resolved by a conference in Rio de Janeiro in January of 1963. We will not attempt to resolve this controversy or to map out a way of dealing with inflation but will try to develop guidelines for a financial institution, such as a development bank, to follow during an inflation or in anticipation of one. However, it will help us to know a bit more about the process of inflation.

Inflation is usually defined as a condition in which the financial resources of a country are greater than the current market value of its real resources. If a country has no shortage of foreign exchange, inflationary pressures are likely to spill over into increased imports. If government measures are taken to protect shrinking foreign currency (and they tend to be necessary in such a situation), the pressure is diverted inward, and the result is likely to be increased prices.

We recognize that inflation has many causes. It is usually either demand-led or caused by a cost-price push. In the former variety, an increase in the money supply from whatever cause, often due to a budgetary surplus or to incomes earned during the development of infrastructure, or long-term industrial projects, finds itself chasing after the existing stock of goods and services, and by thus causing their prices to rise, initiates the spiral of inflation.

In the cost-push variety of inflation, external circumstances such as the decline in export earnings experienced in many countries, especially in Latin America over the last decade, cause a balance of payments problem and require a restriction of imports. Since supplies of some goods cannot easily be increased, their cost rises, causing not increased

14

output but increased prices. Rigidities within the country which cause these inelasticities of domestic supply are in many cases due to systems of land tenure, labor immobility, low level of capital used in the process of production, and monopolies. A new problem which has been recently imposed upon developing economies is the power and strength of labor unions, which have been able to get increased wages in spite of the absence of increases in productivity. These increases have then, in many cases, been passed on to the consumer.

Institutions which plan to lend, even in countries which presently enjoy monetary stability, should protect themselves against possible changes in the level of prices.

Inflation, by raising domestic prices, tends to worsen the country's position in the world market for the commodities that it might otherwise export. At the same time, goods from abroad which presumably have not increased in price are more attractive than ever. The resultant pressure on a country's stock of foreign exchange sometimes causes governments to raise the price of foreign currency by devaluing its own.

Since inflation is present and has been present over a significant period of time in many of the developing countries, especially in the countries of Latin America, such as Chile, Brazil, and to some extent, Argentina, and because the very fact of development and the very process of development has a tendency to generate the kinds of forces within a society that can initiate an inflationary spiral and thus jeopardize an unprotected lender, let us investigate in some detail the measures and policies that a development bank might take to protect itself against the possibility of an increase in domestic prices, or against the possibility of an increase in the price of foreign currencies.

INFLATION INTENSIFIES THE NEED FOR DEVELOPMENT BANKING

Capital Gap Widens

At the present time, in many of the developing countries where there is a critical shortage of funds for medium- and long-term investment, commercial banks frequently do not prevent their borrowers from investing in short-term loans in fixed assets with the implicit or stated agreement

that the loan will be renewed. These short-term loans are
then "rolled over" and renewed from time to time.

And, quite naturally, commercial banks, which obtain
their principal source of funds from short-term demand deposits, take a considerable risk when they permit a borrower
to make an investment which cannot be converted into cash
within a short time.

Inflation increases the risk of term investments, and as
a consequence, commercial banks are even less likely to
acquiesce to a borrower's making fixed investments with
short-term funds. Thus, the lack of medium- and long-term
investment funds in a country becomes even more serious
and the need for a development bank even greater.

Capital Market Worsens

By heightening uncertainty, inflation may inhibit the buy-
ing and selling of debt or equity instruments. However, inflation at the same time causes money to lose some of its
attributes of liquidity and causes potential investors either to
invest abroad or to invest in unproductive domestic assets,
such as land, luxury, housing, inventory, and the like.

A development bank, if it operates in such a way as to
generate the confidence of the investing public, might well
attract some of these investment funds, even in an inflation,
into equity shares or, if proper protection is offered, debt
instruments in productive enterprises. Indeed, the dis-
tinguished Brazilian economist and political figure, Roberto
de Oliveira Campos, has commented on Brazil's inflation as
weeding out investors who were not willing to take a risk.
The existence in Brazil of a number of smoothly functioning
development finance institutions has quite likely contributed
to and facilitated the economic growth that, until recently,
Brazil enjoyed even during severe inflation.

Foreign Private Capital Flows Shrink

Development bankers well know that an inflation, or the
threat of an inflation, is a severe inhibitor of an inflow into
a developing country of private foreign investment. A development bank, however, with its international financial
contacts and with a record of sound financial business

judgment may be able to induce an increase or prevent a
decrease in this flow, in spite of inflation.

Uncertainty Affects Domestic Entrepreneurs

Inflation and the uncertainty it brings probably cause
domestic entrepreneurial talent to continue to invest in commerce or in speculation. Even though, in a normal inflationary situation, equity investment might be expected to keep
pace with the increase of domestic prices, entrepreneurs
who are not accustomed to investment in production may be
reluctant to venture into this field. A development bank, if
it establishes itself on a sound financial base and if it gains
the confidence of this entrepreneurial talent, may be able, in
spite of an inflation, to help to eliminate this reluctance
to make a permanent contribution to productivity.

For these reasons, a development bank is potentially extremely useful in a country even during an inflation. Put
another way, the gaps and bottlenecks to economic growth
which a development bank is especially designed to fill become even more acute during periods of rising prices. We
do not mean to imply that a development bank can or should
be initiated during such a period. Indeed, we try to point
out the problems involved during inflation in both organizing
and operating such a bank.

INFLATION, THE SOLVENCY OF A DEVELOPMENT BANK, AND THE MAINTENANCE OF VALUE OF ITS ASSETS AND LIABILITIES

The threat which inflation poses to a development bank
with respect to its balance sheet is really of two kinds, depending upon the nature of the bank's liabilities. If these
liabilities are repayable in a foreign currency (its loans and
investments), the bank may be thrown into bankruptcy by a
devaluation.

If, on the other hand, its liabilities are denominated in
local (domestic) currency, inflation reduces assets and liabilities proportionally. The threat of bankruptcy is not present, but inflation threatens the bank's effectiveness and even
its existence as a financial institution. With prices rising,
as we pointed out above, lenders of fixed sums are injured
in an inflation to the extent that when they receive back their
fixed sum after the lending term, it commands less real

resources than when the sum was lent. Thus, without protection, loan funds vanish, both as sources and uses of development bank funds.

One analyst unofficially calculated for the Industrial Development Bank of Turkey at one stage of its growth when it
had obligations repayable in dollars (although it was never
unprotected) that a 10 per cent devaluation of the lira could,
if the bank were unprotected, wipe out one year's profit;
that a 25 per cent devaluation would wipe out the accumu-
lated profits and the reserves of previous years; and that a
75 per cent devaluation would completely decapitalize
the bank. This example illustrates the need for a term
lender, even when he is lending in an economic situation of
stable prices, to protect himself against the possibility that
the value of his assets may decline while the value of his
liabilities remains the same. Equally important, in the case
that both assets decline proportionally, is the requirement
that the development banker protect himself against loss of
value of his assets. Most important of all is that both the
lender and borrower be aware of the implications of inflation on the loan, that they assess the likely impact of inflation and take steps to protect themselves if necessary.

Inflation and devaluation are inextricably linked. The
relationship is probably one to one in the long run. But, in
the short and medium term, they may not be proportional to
one another. Indeed, there is evidence, presented in Table
1, Page 21, that devaluation lags behind in domestic price
increases and that, in the short and medium term, domestic
prices are likely to rise more than the price of foreign exchange. The table, however, was calculated using official
rates of exchange. If free market rates were used, the statistics might reflect a closer correlation between the two.
A business which requires foreign exchange can never be
sure what price it will have to pay when foreign exchange
allocations are under government control.

The close relationship between changes in domestic
prices and changes in the price of foreign exchange is due
principally to two reasons: First, a rise in domestic prices
makes foreign imports more attractive, especially imports
which substitute for domestic goods the prices of which have
risen. Increased demand for imports augments the demand
for foreign exchange. Second, rising domestic prices

decrease the competitive position of a country's exports vis-a-vis the World Market and tend to lower the total value, in the absence of inelasticities of demand, of a country's foreign exchange earnings. Thus, the increase in demand for foreign exchange plus a shrinkage or, at least, a potential shrinkage of foreign exchange availability augments the pressure on the country to increase its price. If foreign exchange were freely fluctuating, the increase in demand plus restriction of supply would naturally and normally cause a rise in the price of foreign exchange.

Development bankers concerned with the price of foreign exchange should watch carefully the posture of the International Monetary Fund and of local government officials to ascertain likely corrective measures when faced with shrinking foreign exchange reserves and rising domestic prices. The International Monetary Fund sometimes would seem to be pursuing mutually conflicting monetary objectives of maintaining both exchange rate stability and convertibility. Very often, in order to achieve convertibility, the Fund must permit the country to devalue its currency. IMF will usually permit a country to devaluate its currency only if it takes internal measures, such as domestic austerity, balanced budget, etc., calculated to insure stable prices.

Because of the uncertainty that surrounds foreign exchange availabilities, and because of the fact, mentioned above, that having liabilities denominated in foreign exchange poses a potential threat to the solvency of the bank, a development bank should limit its foreign exchange borrowings to its actual foreign exchange requirements. It should try to obtain local currency for all domestic requirements. Local currency is sometimes available from private local sources, from local government budgets, and from such lenders as the Inter-American Development Bank and the Agency for International Development.

But the problem of maintaining the value of the assets of a development bank is crucial in the threat or in the existence of an inflation, no matter whether the loan is to be made in local or foreign currency. The issue to be decided in each particular commitment of funds made by the development bank is: How is the risk of maintenance of value to be borne or shared? The following alternatives may be open to a development bank:

Equity Investment

One recommendation to a development banker who might be faced with an inflation is to shift his resources into equity. More specific details are given below as to the kind of project to be selected (both for lending and for equity investment) during an inflation. However, equity investment is usually only a limited alternative to a development banker. Very few bankers would advise that equity investments be made with borrowed funds, and indeed most lines of credit extended to development banks from international lending agencies prohibit the use of these lines of credit for equity investment. The World Bank, however, in several cases, permitted its lines of credit to be used for equity investment. Nevertheless, a development bank is usually limited in its ability to make equity investments to the extent to which it itself has received equity capital.

It might be explored, in the light of the World Bank precedent mentioned above, that a development bank might be permitted by the international lender to take either equity or at least debt positions with a convertibility feature to be exercised only upon consultation with the financial organization concerned. Such positions would enable the development bank to convert debt to equity to protect its investment.

Maintenance of Value Burden Borne by Bank

It is conceivable, of course, that the intermediate credit institution, the development bank itself, might bear the risk of inflation. Naturally, in countries where prices and exchange rates remain stable, a development bank may conveniently bear this burden without any harm. Banks in the United States, for example, bear this risk without fear.

However, one can see at a glance that from Table 1 on Page 21 chances are that development will sooner or later exert an upward pressure on prices. We have seen above, in the mock calculations done for the Industrial Development Bank of Turkey, that devaluation can decapitalize a bank very quickly. It has been the experience of development bankers in the past that a development bank seriously jeopardizes its viability if it attempts to undertake the risk of maintaining the value of its assets itself.

Table 1

The Course of Inflation in Selected
Latin American Countries from 1959 to 1963

	% Inflation in Terms of Price of Foreign Exchange, 1959-63	% Inflation in Terms of Price of Foreign Exchange Per Year	% Inflation in Terms of Local Purchasing Power, 1959-63
Peru	none	none	30.9
Argentina	59	11.8	129
Brazil [1]	359	71.0	399
Chile	283 [2]	56.0 [2]	97
	103 [3]	20.0 [3]	
Colombia	40 [4]	8.0 [4]	53
Ecuador	20 [3]	4.0 [3]	15
	9 [2]	2.0 [2]	
Uruguay	48 [5]	12.0 [5]	125
Venezuela	0	0	0.95

[1] Implicit exchange rate based on exports from 1959-63. No effective exchange rate is available due to the existence of multiple rate schedules for various categories of commodities.

[2] Free Market.

[3] Official Market.

[4] Principal selling rate. No effective exchange rate is available due to the existence of multiple rate schedules for various categories of commodities.

[5] No effective exchange rate available before 1960, and no implicit exchange rate available due to lack of records of transactions. Hence, this effective exchange rate is calculated for four years only (1960-63).

Source: IMF statistics for cost-of-living figures and exchange rates.

There are, however, ways in which this can be done, and they may be more or less appropriate in a given institutional or political circumstance. The use of an interest surcharge on the loans that a bank makes, such surcharge feeding into a reserve for maintenance of value, is thought by most experts not to be sufficient to protect fully a bank during an inflation. This is especially true when the development bank is being organized and will be initiated during an inflation. Such a reserve fund might have a chance of accumulating enough to guard against depreciation or inflation, if it had a long period of stability that preceded the period of inflation and if the inflation were mild and short-lived.

The technique of using an interest surcharge as a protection against inflation or devaluation is not recommended for a private institution. A public institution, however, might, for political reasons, undertake the financial burden itself with or without an interest surcharge. In this case, it could probably count on a subsidy from the government, if such a subsidy were required by inflation or depreciation. Or, if some of its borrowers were engaged in export operation, it might be able to arrange conversion of the foreign exchange to local currency at a more favorable rate.

It is conceivable that a public or private institution might undertake the responsibility for being a self-insurer against depreciation or inflation if the government would make a long-term, low-interest or no-interest loan, or transfer the administration of a special fund to the institution for the general purposes of its operation with the proviso that the income from administering this fund would go into a special reserve for possible loss through inflation. In this case, for the government to set aside or create this fund, it would by this act be indicating such confidence in the institution, in the job that it was capable of performing in this society, and that the institution might be thus assured of additional assistance if inflation or depreciation depleted this reserve.

In the main, however, a development bank, especially a private development bank, is ill-advised to assume this risk itself. Indeed, the International Finance Corporation requires, as a condition of a credit to, or an investment in, a development bank, that the problem of maintenance of value be solved to its satisfaction. This usually means that the bank will take steps to pass the risk either to the government or to the sub-borrowers.

Maintenance of Value Risk Passed on to Borrower

The usual method of handling the problem of maintenance of value in the past has been for a development bank to pass the risk to the sub-borrower. That is:

a. the sub-borrower receives the loan denominated in dollars or denominated in some other foreign currency likely to remain stable throughout the period of the loan; or

b. the loan has been tied to a domestic index such as that of prices, wages, or cost of living; or

c. the loan has been tied to a commodity; or

d. other attempted solutions such as shortening the repayment period or requiring participations in profits and earnings.

The reason behind passing the loan on to the sub-borrower is that passing the risk in this manner distributes it over the entire range of bank lending. One therefore has, instead of the development bank itself taking one large risk, a lot of smaller borrowers taking a more widely distributed and much smaller risk. Another reason is that many people feel that the sub-borrower's control over the price of a final product is sufficient for him, in the case of an inflation, to pass this price increase along to the ultimate consumer.

a. Tie Loan to Stable Foreign Currency

Tying the loan to a unit of foreign currency, such as the dollar, has been a method of protection used by some banks, including the Industrial Development Bank of Israel. Where a bank's liabilities are denominated in dollars, its assets, according to some observers, should be in dollars too. The maintenance of value burden is thus shifted from the bank to the sub-borrower.

In such a case, the sub-borrower undertakes a

certain amount of local currency denominated in dollars or some other stable currency. When he pays back the loan, his amortization schedule is adjusted to a local currency requirement adapted to repay to the development bank local currency equivalent in value to the amount of foreign currency borrowed.

The acceptance of a responsibility of this kind can be extremely dangerous for the borrower. For example, in one case, a borrower from the Industrial Development Bank of Israel found that the principal amount of his loan increased significantly when Israel devalued her currency. Since his loan was tied to the dollar, a technique which is called linkage, the principal of the loan was revised upward to reflect the depreciation. When the firm's officials worked through their financial figures on the basis of the new amount of the loan, they found that the production break-even point was above the capacity of the corporation.

The alternative of raising the price of the product was not open to them in view of government price controls. Thus, the business was squarely up against the alternatives of either declaring bankruptcy or extending themselves even more into debt to obtain machinery which would bring their production above the break-even point. They were able, through the willingness of the IDB, to increase their loan to pursue the latter course; the profit squeeze illustrates the danger involved.

There is another disadvantage to tying the loan to the dollar which is being illustrated now in some Latin American countries where Communist propaganda points out that the economy, in tying its future to the dollar, is becoming overly dependent on the United States. They take every opportunity to point out the weakening in the dollar and also the dangers to national sovereignty that are implicit in financial control by another nation. Linking is not intended to provide any measure of United States control over the borrower or the sub-borrower. Yet, this technique furnishes fodder for the Communist conflagration.

Another drawback to the borrower results from denominating a loan of local currency in dollars. Some borrowers who have only a local currency requirement do not like to see the principal and interest on their loan tied to an outside currency. It gives them a feeling of excessive dependence upon something over which they have no influence or control.

b. Tie Loan to a Commodity

There has been some experience in the use of a loan denominated in terms of a commodity. Such a loan is a partial reflection of the fact that, during an inflation, money loses many of its essential attributes: that of liquidity, that of being a store of wealth, and that of being a standard of deferred payment. For example, in order for Cooperativa Sodimac of Chile to obtain debt capital, it offered bonds denominated in terms of steel, such bonds to carry an interest rate of 7 per cent. The denomination of the bond issue in terms of steel was an incentive to the lender to make the loan.

Also, in Chile, there is an attempt to link the price of land sold through the Corporación de Reforma Agraria and the Instituto de Promoción Agraria to a certain quantity of a staple grain, in this case, wheat. The present value of the land at the time it is sold to the campesinos is denominated in terms of quintals of wheat. The principal amount of the loan is re-evaluated at periodic intervals during the life of the loan and readjusted upward if there is any change in the price of this commodity.

The risk of loss of earning power (interest income), through devaluation or inflation, is shared by the bank with the borrower in the following manner: One half of the interest charge is payable to the lender without any adjustment at the agreed-upon rate, and the other half of the interest charge is scaled upward if necessary according to any increase in the price of wheat.

Linkage of a loan to a commodity is an objective standard about which there can be no question. In

France, several utilities have issued bonds indexed to commodities or services. In one case, a utility company tied the bond to electricity rates. In another, a railroad tied its bonds to government-controlled railroad fares.

Also, there is an element of equity involved in the choice of the commodity to which the loan will be tied. In the Chilean case outlined above, the choice was wheat because this was the principal crop grown on the land sold to the campesinos under the program. The choice of wheat also permitted the farmer to identify a little bit more closely with the equity of the situation. It is a lot easier to explain to a campesino who has limited formal education that his loan will be adjusted in accordance with the increases in the prices he might obtain from his wheat than it is to explain to him that the loan will be adjusted upon changes in the relationship between his currency and the currency from another country.

Drawbacks to the use of the commodity link, in spite of its objectivity, is that, depending upon its market structure, it may not be a good measure of inflation. It is precisely for this reason that a composite of goods and service prices is used as a price index rather than a single commodity.

c. Tie Loan to a Domestic Price Index

Another way for the bank to shift the maintenance of value to the borrower is for it to make the principal and interest charge readjustable at periodic intervals to a particular appropriate domestic index of prices. There are a number of alternative in indexes from which to choose, such as cost-of-living index, a wage or remuneration index, or an index of wholesale prices. The choice would depend upon the resolution of a number of important problems with respect thereto.

Perhaps the most important problem is to determine the type of index that is both fair and feasible for use in making readjustment. Certain indexes of the present cost of living, such as the consumer price

index or the wholesale price index, are fair both to the
borrower and the lender under some circumstances,
as long as they are accurate and impartially calculated. In spite of the difficulties in calculating this
index, in assigning weights, in readjusting according
to quality changes in the market basket, and in obtaining accurate statistics, this index is perhaps the
most appropriate measure of inflation.

However, the cost-of-living index was not chosen
for use in the Chilean savings and loan scheme. The
Krooth-Courshon study, done at the instigation of Mr.
Harold Robinson, then chief of the Housing Division in
the AID mission to Chile, and presently Director of
the Housing Section of the Institutional Development
Division in the Bureau for Latin America, Agency for
International Development, rejected the cost-of-living
index because it did not have a sufficiently direct and
immediate relationship to earnings. Borrowers, who
were wage earners and who would use the money
through the savings and loan scheme to purchase or
build a house, might be unable to make increased payments if payments were adjusted on the basis of an
index of the cost of living.

The index selected, therefore, was a wage index.
Wages, however, may change for several reasons:
(1) because the cost of living has gone up; or (2) because production per worker (productivity) has gone
up; or (3) because labor power has increased to the
extent that labor unions force a redistribution of
income.

In order to adjust for changes in productivity, it
was proposed that the wage index be reduced by changes in per capita production. But this adjustment assumes that wage changes are proportional to changes
in per capita production - an assumption the accuracy
of which is dependent upon the strength of labor
unions.

It was, however, the opinion of Messrs. Krooth
and Courshon that a wage index would bear, over a
period of time, a steady relationship to changes in the
cost of living. If a bank feels that a wage index should

be used, but is afraid that there will be a significant non-cost-of-living component to future wage rises, it is possible to agree with borrowers and/or depositors to adjust their loan or deposit according to either the wage index or the cost-of-living index, whichever is lower.

One of the basic objectives underlying this and any other effort to preserve the assets of a development bank during conditions of price instability is to return confidence to the lender that the real value of the money he lends can be preserved even during an inflation.

The other side of the coin, that is, preserving the real value of money saved by depositors is no less important. The Chilean savings and loan scheme required the readjustment annually of both the aggregate savings and the principal balances on mortgages based on a modification of an index of wages. The index apparently used was the average annual increase of wages and salaries and was prepared by the Servicio Nacional de Estadistica y Censos.

There are a number of potential drawbacks to the use of the remunerations index which must be pointed out at this time. From the standpoint of the borrower, the use of the unadjusted wage index would work a hardship since it would cause the loan to be readjusted upward even if the wage index reflected a wage increase due to increase in productivity, or due to an increase in bargaining strength. From the standpoint of the lender, an index of wages might be disadvantageous since it very often lags behind changes in the cost of living. Rigidities of one kind or another, the varying strengths of local labor unions and the nature of their contracts with employers will modify this situation in individual cases. But, by and large, experience has been that wage rates, as a rule, rise more slowly than cost of living, or at least if they rise at the same rate, they do so with a constant lag.

There is another factor which may be pointed out at this time in the case of a bank's using this method to readjust both the amount of its assets and the amount of its liabilities by means of this index. If the volume of resources in the bank is, say, 100 units of currency, the volume of its loans, leaving a prudent 20 per cent for liquidity reserves, would be 80 units of currency. If the volume of its deposits, which are liabilities to the bank, were adjusted upward according to the basis of an index and the volume of its loans were adjusted upward on the basis of the same index, we would have an adjustment to the figure of 100 and an adjustment to the figure of 80. There would be presumably no adjustment to the 20 units of currency which the bank felt necessary to keep on deposit for liquidity. The cost, therefore, of this differential would be presumably, in the absence of any special arrangement, borne by the bank. This is a cost which might very well be taken care of by a surcharge on the loan, such surcharge to be used for a reserve to reimburse the bank in case of any loss incurred.

From many standpoints, an index of prices is an important tool for a development bank to use to readjust its assets and liabilities. However, one must keep in mind that it is not the index itself, but both borrower and lender confidence in the index which permits it to be useful. In many countries, political considerations influence changes in the price index, and to the extent that they do, the index then loses much of its usefulness.

In Chile, as mentioned above, there have been some experiments with tying assets and liabilities of certain financial institutions to an index of prices (the wage index). However, many feel that the price index is not a reliable measure of price changes. In Mexico, the Mexican Oil Company, PEMEX, issued a price index bond that was outstanding for three or four years. During that period, the price index went up, but the price of oil products did not rise as much, and PEMEX recalled the issue to avoid a greater loss.

Confidence of both borrowers and depositors in the index is one of the most important conclusions which can be drawn from the above. If the bank chooses to use an index, it should endeavor in every way possible to verify beforehand the integrity of the index calculating agency and make an assessment of borrower and lender confidence in the index as a measure of prices.

d. Other Methods of Shifting the Maintenance of Value Burden to the Borrower

There have been other schemes to shift the burden of maintenance of value to the borrower; however, there is very little information as to their effectiveness. One, as mentioned above in the section on "Equity Investment," is to insist on the right to convert debt into equity. Such an option would be exercised by a development bank in the case that inflation had so diminished the real value of the loan that greater value would be realized by converting to equity and selling. This approach can be dangerous especially with respect to liquidity, since in many developing countries the capital market is not well developed and since, in periods of inflation, uncertainty is likely to make the capital market function even more cautiously. However, it is potentially useful: In an inflation one might presume that the value of investments in land, machinery, plant, etc. will keep pace in value with rising prices. Since equity represents a share in these assets, it would presumably also keep pace with rising prices.

Other techniques are accelerated amortization schemes, profit sharing, or provisions for the issuance of bonus shares. The Caisse Central of France requires accelerated amortization of a long-term loan if the borrower's gross sales rise above the figures shown in the financial forecasts, which accompany the loan application, for all loans for more than ten years. After the fifth or sixth year, Caisse requires that the borrowers increase the amount of each installment by one third to one half of the excess of actual sales over forecasted sales. The Government Development Bank of Puerto Rico reserves the right in the case of machinery and equipment loans to require up to one half of the borrower's profit, net of debt service, to be used to repay the loan.

Loans from the former Indonesian State Bank for Industry often combine debt instruments with profit sharing arrangements. As a hedge against inflation, such schemes can be partially or wholly successful, depending upon their terms and conditions. Against a severe inflation, it is highly probable that they would not indemnify the bank completely against loss.

e. Plan of the Chile Cooperative Finance Institute

The Chile Cooperative Finance Institute (IFICOOP) is acutely aware that the maintenance of value problem is one of the most significant problems that it will face. This bank which was organized in 1964 and began operations in the fall of 1965 is a part of the Inter-American Cooperative Finance System.

In its loan application to AID for an initial capital loan, the bank staff first outlined several criteria for such an index. First, it must be of general application; second, it must be in accordance with the payment capacity of the borrower; and third, it must permit the financier to maintain his purchasing power and avoid his decapitalization.

The following plan worked out by the Board of Directors of IFICOOP is thought to be the most imaginative approach to the problem encountered, to date, by the author.

(i) Loans with readjustment clauses should be made from the following sources of funds:

(1) IFICOOP's own capital;

(2) savings allocated to the members;

(3) local currency obtained from foreign sources;

(4) local currency obtained from local sources if readjustment is a part of the agreement by which the resources are obtained;

(5) loans of foreign currency from any source.

(ii) <u>Loans which might be made without a readjustment clause</u> from the following sources
of funds:

   (1) IFICOOP's reserves;

   (2) term deposits from cooperatives which
are not readjustable;

   (3) local currency from foreign sources
which are not readjustable;

   (4) local currency from local sources which
are not readjustable.

Even though they did not want to work with an
excessive number of indexes, the bank was anx-
ious to have an equitable system of readjust-
ments. Consequently, its plan calls for the use
of a number of readjustment measures as follows:

(i) <u>Tie loan to dollar</u>: Dollar-tied loans will
only be granted to a cooperative to assist
a project which will result in increased
exports. The increase in export revenue
must be greater than the amortization
payments on the loan.

(ii) <u>Tie loan to wage index</u>: Loans to cooperative
housing projects which are planned to be tied
to a wage index in order to link the repayment
obligation closely with the ability of the borrower to repay.

(iii) <u>Tie loan to consumer price index</u>: For supply
and merchandising cooperatives, savings and
credit organizations, and production and transportation.

(iv) <u>Tie loan to agricultural price index</u>: For loans
to agricultural cooperatives and also rural
electrification societies.

With respect to funds obtained abroad, the
government of Chile has agreed to indemnify the

bank for any difference which may occur due to greater fluctuation in the foreign exchange rate than obtained from the readjustment of the loans.

The bank plans that short-term loans (of less than one year) might be granted at 16 per cent interest if there is no readjustment clause. If there is a readjustment clause, or if the credit is at medium or long term, the interest rate will drop to 6 per cent.

The policy of shifting the maintenance of value burden by the development bank to the sub-borrower has been one of several forces tending to cause development banks to lend solely to large sub-borrowers, whom the bank might presume may have the financial soundness and the financial sophistication to protect themselves against profit squeeze in the case of devaluation or price inflation. Many banks have, for this and other good reasons, established a lower lending limit below which they will not lend.

When a development bank in an inflation passes the maintenance of value burden to a sub-borrower who is faced with price controls, the bank takes a great risk that the borrower might not be able to repay the loan, and that the solvency of the bank itself might thereby be placed in jeopardy.

Shift of Maintenance of Value Burden to Local Government

When a development bank has liabilities denominated in dollars, many feel that local governments should assume a major share of the burden of maintenance of value. When a development bank has liabilities denominated in local currency, there is no prima facie reason why the government should enter the picture at all.

In the former instance, however, because of the clear danger of bankruptcy of the bank in the event of devaluation, the position of the government to control devaluation through action of the central bank, and the power of the government through the use of monetary and fiscal policy to influence the domestic price level, many feel that the government should bear the risk of maintenance of value burden. This argument is made even more forcefully in the case that the financial institution with foreign currency liabilities is relending to small businesses, small farmers, or for production, the price of which is controlled.

Already in Latin America, several governments have been willing to undertake the maintenance of value burden. The government of Colombia is requiring the Instituto Colombiano de Reforma Agraria (INCORA) to repay only the amount of currency borrowed. The Colombian government is also taking a risk in the case of a dollar credit to the Instituto de Credito Territorial. In Ecuador, too, the government seems willing to assume part or all of the risk of maintenance of value of funds borrowed by an intermediate credit institution. In Peru, however, present legislation may not permit the Central Bank to accept this risk. The government of Pakistan, as another example, guaranteed the Pakistan Industrial Credit and Investment Corporation (PICIC) against any loss due to devaluation with respect to an IBRD credit, although it has not done so for recent credits.

In most AID dollar loans, however, to countries of the Near East and South Asia regions, the government does not undertake the burden of maintenance of value for the banks. In a two-step loan to the Industrial Development Bank of Turkey, made by the Agency for International Development, the bank has undertaken to pay to the government of Turkey the amount of the loan over a period of ten years at the rate of 5.5 per cent with maintenance of value. The Turkish government has agreed to repay the loan in dollars to AID at 0.75 per cent over a forty-year period. From the time the loan is made until it is repaid to the Turkish government, the maintenance of value burden is borne by the IDB, which passes it on to its sub-borrowers. Beginning at the time the loan is completely repaid to the government of Turkey until the time that that government is obliged to complete its repayments to AID in dollars, the maintenance of value burden, of course, is borne by the government of Turkey. This kind of a loan is, in fact, two loans: one to the intermediate credit institution at 5.5 per cent for ten years with maintenance of value; and the second to the government of Turkey, at 0.75 per cent for forty years with maintenance of value.

In the case of the particular loan in question, and in the

case of many loans similar to this one, the maintenance of
value burden is passed by the development bank on to the sub-
borrower, usually by the denomination of the sub-loans in
dollars.

In loans to seasoned financially sound intermediate credit
institutions, which are lending to large- or medium-sized industrial borrowers in situations in which the prices of these
borrowers are not controlled, it is perhaps the most equitable
arrangement that the sub-borrower should assume the maintenance of value burden with respect, at least, to dollar or
other foreign currency credits, if not to all credits. However, in the case of young developing institutions, in their
formative years, and in situations in which, for political and
economic reasons, the government wants to have an impact
on the development of indigenous small businesses or upon
agricultural development, or in situations in which the prices
of the products of the borrowers of the bank are controlled,
then it would be wise to explore fully the possibility that
the government would assume part or all of the maintenance
of value risk.

Shift of Maintenance of Value Burden to Foreign Government or International Lender

A development bank may find, in dealing with institutional sources of funds abroad, that it can obtain foreign currency
funds from which the burden of maintaining the value has
been removed by a foreign government or by an international
lender. Such is the case, for example, with local currency
available under certain sections of U.S. Public Law 480, under
which commodities are bought with dollars in the United
States and sold abroad for local currency. This currency,
under some titles of Public Law 480, is available for relending without maintenance of value. Cooley loans, for example, which arise under the authority of Section 104(e) of this
Act, are repayable in local currency without maintenance of
value. Similarly, loans under Section 104(r) which can be
used for the development of other countries (other than the
country in which the funds were generated) do not require
that the value of the loan be maintained. Such a loan was
made in Indian rupees to the Nepal Industrial Development
Corporation.

The U.S. Extended Risk Guarantee Program can be used

to protect the lender but not the borrower from devaluation. Funds loaned by an American investor to a development bank, for example, can be guaranteed by the United States Government, such guarantee covering all risks, in certain instances, up to 75 per cent of the loan. This guarantee protects the lender in that the United States Government guarantees to repay the loan if the borrower defaults. However, this does not protect the borrower against the possibilities that devaluation will eliminate his profits or cause him serious financial loss. This technique, however, will be useful in stimulating the flow of funds to developing countries. An extended risk guarantee may be obtained for less than 2 per cent of the amount being guaranteed.

THE EFFECT OF INFLATION UPON OTHER DEVELOPMENT BANK POLICIES

General

The management of any development bank will want to have in mind the following other reasons in which it may find policies influenced by inflation. Clearly no definite recommendations are possible. Each bank response should be developed, however, in full awareness of the impact of inflation on the particular banking situation and in full awareness of the policy alternatives available.

Interest Rates

Experience in many cases has indicated that a development bank cannot fully protect itself against loss of earnings and decapitalization during severe inflation through the use of interest rates and surcharges on the loans that it makes. However, if the development bank anticipates that it will have a number of years of price stability within which to build up a reserve against loss due to devaluation or inflation, conceivably, it might build up a sufficient reserve to protect itself against loss of capital and earnings.

It is characteristic that, during an inflation, capital becomes scarce and interest rates are quite likely to rise, as a reflection of this scarcity. Corporación de Fomento de la Producción (CORFO) in Chile charges 12 per cent with the rate rising to the legal maximum, around 17 per cent, for overdue loans. Yet, CORFO does not accept the maintenance

of value burden for dollar credits, but rather makes loans
denominated in dollars.

As can be noted in Table 1 on Page 21, in most of the
countries over the period analyzed, an interest rate adjustment would not have been sufficient to indemnify the bank
against loss from either inflation or devaluation.

Prior agreement with a borrower from a development
bank to adjust the rate of interest in a pre-arranged manner,
according to a particular index, or according to some other
equitable arrangement, might be sufficient to protect the
earnings of a bank but not the capital of a bank. During an
inflation, rising costs have probably increased the costs of
operation of the bank. Salaries are likely to have gone up.
Supplies and other elements of the cost of operations of a
development bank will have gone up too. Unless income is
adjusted, the bank will be caught in a squeeze between fixed
earnings and rising costs. Reduced earnings will jeopardize
the ability of the bank to raise additional capital or to add to
its staff necessary technical competence or, indeed, to perform many of its development functions.

We mentioned above, in the case of land sales by Instituto de Promoción Agraria in Chile, an example of adjustment of 50 per cent of the interest charge. This charge is
adjusted upward according to an index of wheat prices. This
measure did not fully protect the development bank against
loss of earning power due to inflation. The other 50 per cent
was in this case borne by the bank. Some linkage, between
the rate of interest charged by the bank on its loans and the
rate of increase in prices, is therefore desirable. The precise relationship, of course, will depend upon the portfolio
of the bank and the conditions of its investments, upon the
bank's earning capacity and financial soundness, and upon
possible legal impediments.

With reference to the latter, many international lenders
and foreign national lenders, in some cases because of con-
gressional pressure, limit the maximum interest rate that
a development bank may charge. In many cases, there is
legislation which fixes maximum interest rates. In such a
case, a bank should press for flexibility so that it can have
maximum array of tools with which to deal with inflation,
but in the interim, it should pursue other methods of

protecting itself.

Term of Lending

A development bank can protect itself to some extent in an inflation by shortening its term of lending, forcing the borrower to renegotiate the loan intermittently, at which time new cost-price relationships may be examined and the loan or the interest rate adjusted accordingly. Banco Agrícola do Espiritu Santo in Brazil, for example, shortened the normal five-year tractor loan to two or three years because of the existing inflation in Brazil.

Some development banks have arranged with their borrowers to shorten the repayment period and accelerate repayment of the loan if profits or earnings reach a certain ratio, as they might do in the case that an inflation generates windfall profits. Such profits are made by many manufacturers who, in anticipation of price increases, store up on raw materials and then manufacture and sell their products after the prices have gone up. Inflation in this case can be seen as disguising cost-price relationships and can very often insulate high-cost producers from the competitive market. This method of shifting the maintenance of value burden to the borrower has been discussed on Page 30 and need not be repeated.

A development bank has to beware of the possibility that, by shortening its term, the bank may be ignoring or increasing the medium- and long-term credit gap which it was created to fill.

Security Requirements

In general, the attitude of a development banker toward security is likely to be slightly different from that of a commercial banker. A commercial banker, who is a short-term lender and who has a requirement for a certain amount of liquidity, is likely to look very closely at the security taken in return for a loan and his ability to sell it in order to pay off the loan if necessary. To obtain security, a development banker, because his lending is usually for a longer term, must rely, for the most part, upon the viability of the project for which he is lending. This is not true in some agricultural development banks and in some cooperative banks which are also lending for short terms but for productive projects. However, even in these instances, the development bank is best advised to focus as sharply upon the viability of the project as upon the security taken.

In spite of such focus, security must not be ignored by a development banker. In an actual inflation or in the anticipation of one, the security selected must be capable of maintaining its value. Generally, even in times of stable prices, a development banker will lend no more than 50-60 per cent of the value of the assets which secure the loan.

Banks for cooperatives in the United States can lend up to 75 per cent of the value of unhedged commodities and have the authority to lend for operating capital purposes without taking security. In practice, they seldom lend without taking security, but sometimes do lend up to 100 per cent of the current value of warehoused commodities.

Probably the best hedge against inflation is for the bank to take designated commodities as securities. These commodities presumably would be located in a warehouse and would not be released except upon permission of the lender. In case of default on the loan, these commodities can probably be sold at increased prices. It would be wise also, during inflation, to increase margins slightly, especially if the prices of the commodities taken in security were subject to government regulation.

Land also, in some cases, may be used as a hedge against inflation. Machinery, buildings, and other fixed assets are acceptable as security during an inflation if there is a reasonable chance that their value will be maintained and that they may be able to be sold for an amount sufficient to cover the loan. A floating lien on commodities, such as might be taken by a lender to a market or some other retail store, requires close supervision so that the borrower does not deplete his assets and impair the loan. However, in an inflation, there is nothing wrong with taking such a lien if supervision can insure that the borrower does not impair the security for the loan.

Investment Policies

A development bank, depending upon the kind of a bank

that it is, may find itself with a greater or lesser amount of idle funds on its hands. If the development bank is also a bank of deposit, it may find itself with funds that it has not loaned, especially funds that have been committed but not disbursed. During periods of stable prices, the holding of assets in money form or in near-money such as low-yielding government bonds is a sensible investment. But, during inflation, as noted above, money loses some of its aspects of liquidity, including its value as a store of wealth. Therefore, a development bank in an inflation runs a risk that its capital may be impaired to the extent that it holds money or near-money.

It is relevant here to note that a development bank is not likely to have foreign exchange idle since most international lenders disburse only through letters of commitment when the sub-borrower spends committed development bank funds.

However, the development bank is likely to have idle local currency, especially during its initial period. A development bank should investigate forms of investment which are likely to maintain better their value during an inflation. For example, it might discount short-term commercial paper or it might take short-term positions itself.

There are several potential drawbacks to this kind of operation. First of all, there is the possibility that the bank's charter might not permit it to do so. Secondly, the competition with the commercial banking system might arouse a hostility toward the development bank on the part of the commercial banking sector. Thirdly, this safe and remunerative financial activity might absorb too much of the bank's funds. The latter appears to be the case with the Industrial Bank of Syria which, although its founders hoped for it to be a development bank, finds that most of its assets are indeed short-term investments.

Capital Formation

Inflation raises a number of significant problems with respect to the raising of capital by a development bank. During an inflation, it was noticed in the case of the Investment Development Bank of Turkey that bond sales were not effective and did not succeed. However, an equity offering at the same time was oversubscribed. This is easily understood:

A bond, during an inflation, with its fixed interest and its fixed repayment obligation, depreciates unless some arrangements are made to maintain its value. Equity investment, on the other hand, might reasonably be expected to keep pace with inflation.

We mentioned above a technique used by Cooperativa Sodimac, Ltda., in Chile to make bonds more attractive by tying them to a certain amount of a commodity, in this case, steel.

Whether a development bank intends to obtain its debt capital from time or demand deposits, as is the case for some development banks for cooperatives, or whether it intends to borrow its debt capital by raising bonds or obtaining other loans, it must give assurance to the lender or depositor that inflation will not impair the loan or deposit. As mentioned above, in the case of the capital formation of the savings and loan institutions in Chile, it was necessary to reconstruct the confidence in savings as a form of investment before the institution could be financially successful in raising its capital.

The principles tested in this case undoubtedly hold true for any institution in similar circumstances. In Chile, as mentioned above, the confidence was instilled by tying savings deposits to the same index of wage to which the bank's loans were tied. This insured the saver that the value of his savings would not be impaired by rising prices. Such a technique, or some modification of this technique, should be considered by a development bank during inflation; otherwise, its efforts to obtain debt capital are not likely to be successful.

In development banks for cooperatives, an interesting capitalization technique has been devised and tested in the United States for the raising of equity. A borrower from such a bank is required to set aside a surcharge on interest of between 10-25 per cent of his interest charge for the purchase of stock in the development bank. When the bank's authorized capital has been reached, the purchases of stock by new borrowers act in such a manner as to retire the capital stock of the bank on a first-in-first-out basis, serving thereby to revolve the capital and insuring that the bank will be owned by current borrowers.

DEVELOPMENT BANK PROJECT APPRAISAL AND SELECTION DURING AN INFLATION

Project Selection

In spite of a shortage of viable projects, a development banker during an inflation may be able to exercise his judgment with respect to project selection in such a way as to insulate him better from the dangers inherent in inflation and devaluation.

Evidence presented in Table 1, Page 21, tends to show that domestic prices will rise more during an inflation than the price of foreign currency in the inflating country. There is other evidence to the effect that devaluation and inflation in the long run will be proportional. Over a medium-term period, however, it is more likely that domestic prices will rise by more than the price of foreign exchange. If inflation and devaluation were the only operant forces with which the development banker would have to contend, assuming the development bank has no significant amount of debt repayable in foreign currency, and assuming there are no government controls on foreign exchange, he would, to maximize short-run profits, select:

a. Projects with Substantial Import Component

Such a project would tend to have a stable cost structure presuming that prices abroad were not affected by the rise in domestic prices, and yet might be able to sell internally at rising prices. If the product were exported, then it would also be an advantage to have a substantial import component the price of which is stable.

A serious drawback to be considered here is that very often a balance of payment constraint requires a country to take measures to control foreign exchange. Among these measures are: devaluation, which makes imports more expensive and exports cheaper; quotas, which may limit the absolute amount of imports of inputs to the project; multiple exchange controls, which may seriously affect importation of project components; and restrictive licensing arrangements, in which the project may not obtain a license to buy from abroad at all.

The way the government is likely to react during a balance of payments crisis, or during a time of reduced foreign exchange availability, must be carefully considered by a development bank before selecting a project which has a substantial import component. Countries that have switched from a system of multiple exchange rates to a single valued rate are not likely to return to the multiple system and are certainly not encouraged to do so by the International Monetary Fund. Countries in such a position are likely to use the technique of devaluation or perhaps quotas or licensing arrangements as controls over the availability of foreign exchange.

b. Projects Whose Products Are Consumed Domestically

Such projects will be able to sell in a market of rising prices. If the project were to produce a product to be sold abroad, the prospect of rising costs and stable prices would not be conducive to a healthy profit picture.

c. Projects Whose Products Are Not Subject to Price Control

Many projects involving the sale of agricultural products find themselves in a profit squeeze during inflation because of legal constraints upon price changes. Such projects are not as attractive to a development banker during an inflation as projects the product of which can be increased in price to compensate for rising costs.

d. Projects Which Have Short Gestation Periods

Such projects acquire products quickly and presumably can be implemented through the use of short-to-medium-term loans. Thus, a development banker can move into a project situation and realize his investment before inflation harms the value of the loan.

It may, however, be the case that the development bank will be more concerned with conserving or generating foreign exchange than with short-run profit margins, in which case it should look for projects, ceteris paribus, which have minimum import requirements, and which in turn find a healthy market abroad.

Project Appraisal

Inflation requires that added care be taken by the development bank staff to insure that the relevant aspects of the project are considered. Some relevant considerations are, for example:

a. Have price and cost forecasts presumed any changes in cost of prices? Are these presumptions reasonable in the light of the current and prospective situations?

b. If the product is to be exported, increasing domestic cost will tend to increase price, and the competitive position in the World Market will tend to deteriorate. How important is it to the project to sell abroad? What is the elasticity of demand for the product and what would happen to demand if the price were increased? What chances are there for a domestic market if the foreign market is closed because of increase in price?

c. If a significant percentage of the components of the project need to be imported, domestic inflation will improve the position of this good on the domestic market. How likely is the local government to introduce exchange controls or make existing controls more stringent?

d. A project can seriously be affected by the efforts of a government to restore price stability or restore the competitiveness of her exports upon the World Market through devaluation. How committed is the local government to exchange stability? How likely is the local government to devalue her currency? What are the likely effects of action on the part of the local government to re-introduce price stability?

e. Most projects fail because of deficiencies on the part of management. Specifically in regard to inflation, one might consider the abilities of management to take advantage of rising prices and to act promptly and effectively in the face of impending devaluation. The project analyst should

direct questions specifically at the prospective
manager of a project. Usually a few direct
questions can illuminate management knowledge
of, and prospective competence to handle, these
matters.

IMPLICATIONS FOR THE ORGANIZATION OF A DEVELOPMENT BANK

Some of the suggestions contained herein have implications for the organization of a development bank. In the provisions of a development bank's charter, one must make sure
that the bank can take equity or participate in earnings. Very
often, this charter provision is overlooked or eliminated for
one reason or another. Also, the development banker must
make sure that the bank can take short-term positions with
idle funds. This, indeed, might require changes in the
legislation permitting the bank to operate. Such legislation,
even if unavailable, should be sought.

CONCLUSION

The seriousness of the requirement for a development
banker to relate his operating policies to prospects of rising
prices and devaluation should not be minimized. However,
the problem is not easy to resolve. Most banking experience
in this country has been under a situation of relative price
stability. Bankers in this country are not accustomed to
taking steps to protect the value of their assets during an inflation, nor are they used to using special techniques to cata-
lyze the flow of equity or debt capital. Almost all the debt
contracted by the U.S. banking system is in domestic currency. Although they may be subject to gradual asset depreciation during an inflation, banks, therefore, do not face the
threat of bankruptcy that those which borrow abroad might
face.

Development bankers in countries which have experienced
inflation have seen investment patterns change during periods
of unstable prices, have seen investment move abroad, into
real estate, into inventory, into luxury housing, or even -
and this is perhaps an unwise choice on the part of an invest-
or - into hoards. A development banker in an inflating country has seen foreign private direct portfolio investment flows
cease or become seriously reduced during an inflation or
during a period in which inflation is threatened, and he can be

immediately in full sympathy with the perils of the unprotected lender.

This advice intends to be optimistic and to suggest to a development banker that his institution, if the proper safeguards are taken, can mitigate the impact of the inflation on his balance sheet to a great degree. Although in a severe inflation the structure of a country is so seriously disturbed that a development bank should expect to suffer some impairment, a development banker would hope to end the period as sound as he was when the inflation began.

Prudent development banking during an inflationary period will require that tested measures be taken to protect the development bank against risks of loss during inflation. The risks during an inflation, as pointed out above, are not quite the same if the bank owes a stable foreign currency as when it owes local currency. For full protection, if the bank's debts are in dollars, its assets (loans and investments) should be repayable in dollars or in local currency the amount of which keeps pace with the appreciation of the dollar.

One of the more promising approaches to protecting a bank during a period of inflation involves the concept of sharing the risk of loss during inflation among the various institutions involved. The bank might assume part of the risk by putting a surcharge on its loans, such surcharge feeding into a reserve fund for such contingencies. The sub-borrower might assume part of the risk by using, as his safety valve, control over the prices of his end product. The local government might assume part of the risk using as its source of funds its power of taxation.

But it should be emphasized that no definite course of action during an inflation can be recommended. Such a course is dependent upon the degree of inflation, the past history of inflation, the prospective period of inflation, the financial condition of the bank, and a host of other factors. Even so, it would do well for development bankers who are anticipating conditions of price instability to think through carefully the problems involved in conducting loan operations in an inflation, and derive flexible policies which will be capable of accomplishing the purposes of the bank while, at the same time, protecting it.

Development bankers should seek expert knowledge and advice with respect to the most appropriate combination of policy judgments for an individual bank. Close cooperation is extremely important between the development bank and other institutions, such as commercial banks, investment banks, the central bank, the government finance authorities, etc. Without continuous consultation and cooperation, it is not possible to be prepared to cope with problems which arise during periods of price instability. A development bank should devise ways and means for ensuring continuous contacts in this field.

The points outlined above are not intended to indicate what should be the course of action of a development bank in a given circumstance but to provide a foundation upon which additional thinking may be based and a background upon which specific policy decisions may be established.

3

INTRODUCTION

This study of financing a development bank includes a discussion of the amount of capital needed by a development bank, the proportioning of that capital between debt and equity, and the sources of both of the above kinds of capital for development banks.

INITIAL CAPITAL REQUIREMENTS FOR DEVELOPMENT BANKS

The total capital requirements for a development bank is necessarily limited by both project availability and operating costs. Project availability is a good measure of the upper limits of capital requirements and operating costs is one way of approaching minimum capital requirements.

Upper Limits Of Development Bank Capital

The upper limits of the capital needed by a development bank may be measured by the existence of sound projects ready with little effort for financing. The projects, of course, must lie within geographic areas or fields of activity open to the bank. The shortage of sound projects is the most important problem in the field of development banking, and of course is only a reflection of a number of other important development bottlenecks such as: a shortage of entrepreneurial effort, a shortage of resources, a shortage of technical skill, an unsettling political climate, and cultural values which inhibit or frustrate the drive for material progress, to name a few.

One of the most interesting approaches to the project shortage was the effort of Professor Morris Asimow of UCLA who, in 1961, with support from the Ford Foundation, Pan American Union, the Government of Brazil, and the Agency

48

for International Development among others took a group of graduate students to the hinterlands of Northeast Brazil in the State of Ceara.   There he met with a team from the University of Ceara and together they identified potentially profitable industries, helped to organize interested groups of local citizens into stockholders, helped solicit the subscription of stock, designed the plant, surveyed the market, supervised plant construction and initial operation.   The equity was raised locally from among the many stockholders of each corporation.   The debt was provided by Brazilian development banks, and the projects were prepared by the joint teams and submitted to the development bank for financing.   The effort included most of the usual functions of the traditional "entrepreneur."

This technique has been repeated in four other states in Brazil and could, if properly organized and extended, be of considerable help in meeting the project shortage.

Usually the amount that can be committed to sound projects within two years is the upper limit of a bank's capital requirements.   There are no standard techniques for making such an evaluation and naturally estimates of this upper limit are likely to differ.

This approach was illustrated recently by the pre-bank survey made in the Dominican Republic by Mr. J. Douglas Lawrence of the Inter-American Cooperative Bank Development Program.   A group of cooperative leaders in the Dominican Republic requested the AID Mission for such a survey and, responsive to this request, Mr. Lawrence analyzed a number of cooperative businesses with respect to their operations, markets, managerial capacity and the like.   He found, for example, a shoe manufacturing cooperative which could justify doubling its capital equipment and an improved plant site.   He found a dairy cooperative that needed an additional loan to complete its plant and begin operations. With the knowledge gained from his survey, coupled with his years of experience as a cooperative banker, he was able to make a provisional estimate of the loan volume of the prospective bank.

If there already exist alternative sources of financing for the same kind of projects as fall within the scope of the bank then such an approach as outlined above must make allowance for the possibility that some of the projects will be financed by other means.

One who is analyzing the amount of capital which a development bank might need either in the beginning or for its growth should not overlook any possible sources of information. The analyst must keep in mind, however, that many of the answers he receives may possibly be couched in such a way as to protect the special interest of the person answering the question. Some of the sources of information are as follows:

(a) Existing Manufacturing Industries. What are their own opinions about their own future capital requirements? What are their needs and/or present intentions of expansion? What is their financial condition and quality of management?

(b) Distributive Trades. What are the capital requirements of exporters, importers, merchants, and other service industries in the light of existing conditions of demand and price?

(c) Financial Community. What do bankers say about the prospects for a new development bank? What has been their pace and volume of bank lending? What is the character of their short-term functions through various banking techniques such as rolling over short-term debt, balloon payments, and refinancing, etc.? What is the structure of the capital market and how actively does financial trading take place, if at all?

(d) Development Center, if any. What is their activity and experience within the scope of services that they offer? What kinds of industries have they assisted? What general surveys of investment prospects do they have on file?

(e) Associations of Productive Enterprises. Very often one can get a clear picture of what lies down the road for a particular industry or group of firms by discussing with a trade association its prospects and plans, or its knowledge about trends within the industry.

(f) Government Planning Organizations. There is an increasing tendency in the developing countries to plan
for development. Government ministries related to
planning should have a fairly good idea about the potential of the country for use of funds, for its absorptive capacity and for possible industrial require -
ments. They may even, if they are implementation
oriented, have discussed with a number of businessmen the undertaking of certain industries in fulfill-
ment of the objectives of the plan.

(g) Government Ministries. There are several government ministries which should be able to give some
assistance to the organizing group of a development
bank; such ministries as Industry, Commerce,
Finance, and, in some cases, the Ministry of Planning (if the planning organization has been raised to
a ministerial level) relate more than other government ministries to the problems of economic development and therefore should be in a better position to give sound advice.

There is evidence, especially in Central America, that
capital availability is not the most important constraint upon
industrial and agricultural development. There exist in
many development banks great amounts of excess liquidity,
and significant amounts of unused lines of credit. It does not
injure a bank to have funds in excess of those it is able to lend
because the bank may invest these liquid balances in short-
term earning assets which in turn bring revenue to the bank.
However, in view of the scarcity of medium- and long-term
capital in most developing countries, one can hardly escape
the conclusion that there is probably a higher priority alternative use for such capital.

International and national development financing organizations are not likely to commit funds to a development bank
at any one time in excess of that amount which that particular
bank expects to use within approximately a two-year period.
They much prefer to cover the prospective demand for funds
for two-year periods with the option for the bank to return to
the organization for more funds when necessary.

When IFC plans the financial structure of a development
bank, it tries to insure that there is sufficient equity which,

with debt calculated at a 3:1 ratio, will be sufficient for a
six-year period. The reasoning is simple: Six years is a
minimum period of time for the bank to develop an earnings
record and dividend history which would enable it to go back
to the market for funds.

Development banks have used funds at varying rates of
commitment. For example, the Pakistan Industrial Credit
and Investment Corporation (PICIC) received its first loan
from the World Bank in the amount of $5 million; two years
later, a second loan of double the amount - $10 million. It
came back 21 months later for $15 million, 18 months after
that for $20 million, and 19 months later for $30 million. The
Industrial Development of Turkey similarly has been able to
accelerate its commitment of funds in recent years. After
receiving a loan of $5 million in August of 1964 from IDA,
it came again in March of 1965 for an additional $10 million
and in the interim received a $5 million loan from AID in
November of 1964.

Other development banks, however, have been much
slower than this two-year time period, sometimes for reasons
other than the unavailability of projects. The Industrial Mining and Development Bank of Iran, for example, had committed
by June of 1964 only about 70 per cent of an AID loan of $5.2
million which it received in November of 1959. At the same
time it also received a loan from the World Bank which was
similarly slow of disbursal.

There are several reasons for this slow rate of commitment in addition to the project constraint, among them the
availability of foreign exchange through other sources such as
conversion of local currency, the avoidance in this manner of
such problems as the maintenance value risk, the requirement of sending project details to AID or the World Bank for
review for projects in excess of a certain minimum, the restriction of procurement to the United States (as in the case of
AID loans), and the like. The rate of commitment of loans to
development banks by AID in Latin America has been to date
agonizingly slow. Although there are other facts involved
such as inflation, the project constraint is still significant.

Lower Limits of Development Bank Capital

Development bankers are also often confronted with the

question of what is the minimum total capital needed for a
bank to have a chance to be self-sustaining. One may approach
this problem by consideration of the total resources required
to achieve an earning capacity sufficient to maintain the administration of the bank and to yield a reasonable surplus for
use by the bank either to set aside as reserves, to increase
its services to its customers, or to distribute to its owners
or patrons. This principle is just as sound and as relevant
whether we are talking about industrial stock-owning development banks or development banks for cooperatives. The only
difference in practice between the two is the method of distribution of net earnings. In the former case such earnings
may be returned to stockholders in proportion to their investment. In the latter they are returned to the user-owners
of the bank in proportion to the use made of the financial
facilities of the bank during the period.

Even though it is clear that the total resources available
to the bank for lending are one of the most important determi-
nants of its earning capacity, there are other ways of affecting
earning capacity other than by increasing capital. Any attempt to set a minimum level of resources required for a development bank must be viewed in the light of these other ways
to affect bank earnings. Some of the most important are as
follows:

Spread

A development bank can increase its earnings by increasing the difference between its cost of capital and the interest
rate which it charges its borrowers. Equity capital, of
course, from the standpoint of development bank earnings
is costless. A development bank which was desirous of increasing its earnings would be well advised first to consider
an increase in its equity. As we shall see from "Proportioning
of Capital Between Debt and Equity" (Page 63), however, there
are limits to the acquisition of equity by a development bank.

In the case of stockholder-controlled development banks
one limit on equity rests in the principle of leverage. Prospective return to a unit of equity declines as equity becomes
a greater part of total capital. In the case of user-controlled
development banks (cooperative banks) equity is limited by
capital availability. Cooperatives are by their nature not
capital-attracting businesses, and have always had a difficult

time obtaining equity capital.   Cooperative banks are no
exception.

Cost of capital to a development bank can also be lowered
by the bank's obtaining less expensive funds.   A principal
source of cheap funds for development banks has been host
governments who have desired for one reason or another to
stimulate the growth and strengthening of development banking.   Many governments have made long-term, low-, or
no-interest subordinated loans which have acted as
equity in the capital structure than debt and will be discussed
further in Proportioning of Capital Between Debt and Equity.

Subsidy

Many development banks have in the past been able to
obtain subsidies in one form or another from either local
government or from an international or foreign national lending or technical assistance agency.   Any assistance for which
the bank pays less than market cost is in the nature of a subsidy and by this definition debt acquired by the bank below the
market rate is also a subsidy.

In Ecuador, for example, the Banco de Cooperativas del
Ecuador will receive financial assistance in the form of grants
from AID and from the government of Ecuador which are intended to lessen the strain on the financial structure of the
bank.

An interesting form of quasi-subsidy was granted to the
Industrial Development Bank of Turkey by the government of
Turkey in that they guaranteed 6 per cent dividend on stock of
the bank with payments made by the government under this arrangement regarded as a loan to IDB when made.   This standby arrangement was of inestimable assistance to the bank
when selling its equity shares.

Managed Funds

A frequently used way of increasing the earning capacity
in the formative years of a development bank is to use the
bank as an agency of the subsidizing organization for certain
fiduciary purposes.   For example, in the development of the
Industrial Development Bank of Turkey, the U.S. and Turkish
governments turned over three separate funds to be

administered by the bank at a 3 per cent commission.

Portfolio Transfer

Many development banks had their earnings strengthened by the transfer to the bank of all or part of the portfolio of another banking institution. For example, the Development Bank of Ethiopia received $1 million (Ethiopian dollars) in assets of the Agricultural and Commercial Bank of Ethiopia. The Industrial Mining and Development Bank of Iran received by act of the Iran Parliament in 1959 the entire loan portfolio of the Industrial Credit Bank plus certain loans from the Bank Melli. This portfolio of $18.7 million (equivalent) was transferred to IMDBI on a contract basis as agent of the government for a 3 per cent fee.

Portfolio Management

A development bank can increase its earnings irrespective of its total assets by astute management of its own portfolio. In the initial stages of operation, especially, a development bank may have a sizable amount of uncommitted funds. These funds can be put to short-term use through commercial paper or even as time deposits in commercial banks. In the operating forecast for the Ecuadorean Bank for Cooperatives it was assumed that surplus cash would be deposited at 3 per cent. A bank which plans thus to impair its liquidity for the sake of increasing its earnings would be well advised to negotiate standby credit arrangements with other elements of the banking community.

Cutting Operating Expenses

A development bank should always pay close attention to its operating costs. Its budget forecasting should permit it at all times to see possibilities of increasing earnings through lowering of such costs. In the early operations of a development bank when loan volumes are slow, a development bank which is situated in a community where other business services are available may choose to save on full-time personnel and utilize such competent business services as are locally available such as accounting, engineering specialties, legal facilities, and the like. Even secretarial service can, in some instances, be obtained on a job-contract basis and does not have to be provided for in the full-time staff of a development bank.

Other

There are other ways for a development bank to increase its earnings capacity, through either increasing its income or lowering its expenses, other than by increasing its capital. The Colombia Development Bank for Cooperatives plans to charge an admission fee to new members to amortize administrative costs of the bank. This fee will be 5 per cent of the stock purchase requirement which in turn is 3 per cent of the proposed new members' paid-in capita. Another technique which has been used profitably in some banks is for the bank to charge a fee for technical services to a borrower in connection with either the preparation and submission of a loan application, in connection with problems that might arise during plant start-up and initial operations, or indeed under any other circumstances in which the staff of the bank can make a valuable contribution to the business.

But assuming that the bank will be as prudent and efficient as possible with respect to the above, there still remains the problem of the determination of minimum capital requirements. Let us approach the answer by a consideration of the forecasts of the Ecuadorean Bank for Cooperatives. Table 2 assumes that the interest charged by the bank would be 7 per cent. Some relevant projections are given as follows:

Ecuadorean Bank for Cooperatives
Selected Items, Balance Sheet and Profit and Loss Forecasts
(in 000)

	1	2	3	4	5
1. Capital available at end of year	1006	2024	3057	4108	5169
2. Loans by the Bank	800	1800	3000	4000	5000
3. Interest earnings only	28	91	161	245	315
4. Total Expenses	121	135	154	172	189
5. Net Income* (Loss)	(70.5)	(28.9)	24.5	91	145

*Total Earnings (not shown) minus Total Expenses

Not Official
For Illustration Only

Table 2

Proposed Ecuadorean Bank for Cooperatives
Operating Forecast

Yr. 1 (Yrs. 2-10
to be calculated)

I. Income $40,000

  A. Interest Earned - Loans $28,000
(7% interest rate, no provision for
tax, average outstanding balance)

  B. Interest Earned - Deposits   12,000
(Surplus cash deposited at 3%)

  C. Other Income (Services, etc.)   -o-

II. Expenses 121,555

  A. Interest Paid   7,500
(1) Capital Loan, AID, 3/4%.....   7,500
(2) To purchasers of guaranteed
loans, 5%   -o-

  B. Operating Expenses 105,555

(1) Salaries:	
President(GM)	$24,444
Vice President (Treas.)	11,111
Secretary	8,888
Chief Credit Examiner	13,333
Legal	4,666
Technical Specialist	6,666
3 Secretaries	6,222

(2) Other:	
Directors' expenses	2,555
Travel	3,333
Rent	3,333
Communications	1,666
Depreciation	1,222
Supplies	3,333
Benefits	9,222
Meetings, Ins.	2,500

  C. Provision for Losses on Loans   8,000

III. Net Income (Loss)   Year 1 - ($70,500)

Because cooperatives by their nature are not capital attracting business organizations, debt totalling $5 million in five years comprises most of the capital structure during the early years, before borrower purchases of stock begin to accumulate. Therefore, line 1 above is almost entirely composed of the proposed AID capital loan. However, from year 3 on, equity purchases by members permit the entire amount of the AID loan to be utilized.

One can see that at the end of year 5, income from loans is already significantly greater than total expenses. Before one concludes, however, that $5 million capital will do very nicely for a development bank, one must keep in mind that the cost of this capital is extremely low: 0.75 per cent per annum during the grace period, 2 per cent thereafter. Although the grace period is the principal reason why the gap between income and expenses widens so early, this low-cost capital is one of the principal reasons for the apparent strength of the bank.

A useful rule of thumb that many bankers use when estimating capital requirements of a bank, or when evaluating operation expenses, is that such expenses be 1 per cent of total assets or less. After the fifth year the ratio of operating expenses to total assets for the Ecuadorean Cooperative Bank is forecasted to be 1.9 per cent, and by the end of the tenth year it has dropped to 1.14 per cent. Thus we might conclude that some additional capital could (depending upon the demand, the rate charged and paid by the bank, and the like) give the bank additional earning power with which it might improve this ratio.

In asking the question, "What is the minimum amount of capital that a development bank will need in order to be a viable institution within a five-year period?" let us look at another operating forecast, that of the Colombian Bank for Cooperatives (Table 3). This table assumes that interest charged by the bank would be 10 per cent. Some relevant projections are also given below.

Colombian Bank for Cooperatives
Selected Items, Balance Sheet and Profit and Loss Statement
(in 000)

	1	2	3	4	5
1. Capital available for lending (mostly AID loan)	755	2116	3698	4600	6295
2. Loans by the Bank	650	2086	3564	4450	6000
3. Interest Earned by the Bank	33	137	283	401	526
4. Total Expenses	111	199	236	296	368
5. Total Income* (loss)	(72)	(62)	46	105	158

*Total Earnings (not shown) Minus Total Expenses

In this case, by the end of the fifth year it is planned that this bank will have command over resources equivalent to $6.2 million, composed mostly of the proceeds of an AID $5.7 million loan, plus capital and reserves. In this case, the interest rate used in calculating the cost of capital to the bank was 6 per cent and presumed no subsidy as in the case of Ecuador.

By the end of the fifth year, the ratio of operating expenses to total assets was down to 1.12 per cent and by the end of the tenth year it was predicted to decline to 0.59 per cent.

Clearly, the operating expenses of a development bank play an important role in the determination of capital requirements. In the two examples above, one can see that $5-6 million made available to the bank over a five-year period will do very nicely. Yet is extremely difficult to give precise advice on the operating budget for a development bank during its formative years.

Many operating expense forecasts have presumed the need initially of at least five or six professionals, including a president, vice president, financial or business analyst, engineer, and an accountant. It is usually hoped that at least one of the above has had some legal experience; if not, legal services should certainly be available to the bank if not of its own staff, at least by contract. As one can see in the forecast of the expenses for the Ecuadorean Bank (Table 2), the staff requirements include a president, vice president, secretary, chief credit examiner, legal assistance, and technical specialists. In the Colombian Bank forecast (Table 3) it was not considered necessary in the beginning to have legal services on the permanent staff. In a development bank which plans to invest in industrial projects it is usually found necessary to have a Managing Director, professional assistance in the finance and business analysis function, professional assistance in the technical function, and legal, administrative, and accounting assistance. It is desirable, of course, to plan for the phasing in of additional assistance as workload requires.

The assumptions one makes with respect to operating expenses can make a great deal of difference even though the operating expense forecast for the Ecuadorean and Colombian Banks indicates almost identical personnel requirements. The disparity of almost $50,000 between them indicates different assumptions with respect to salary level. In the Ecuadorean forecast it can be seen that international salaries were used. In the Colombian forecast, however, it was anticipated that sufficient local trained personnel were available, so that a local salary table could be used. Both forecasts, however, were planned with the idea that the Inter-American Cooperative Development Bank Program would provide full-time technical assistance for the first two years of operation, and hence are low by the amount of this assistance, if it is assumed that this assistance would have been obtained by the bank at its own expense if this program were not in existence.

The International Finance Corporation, whose experience in initiating private industrial development banks is extensive, recommends that at the outset competent foreign personnel operate the bank on a management contract or as direct-hire personnel of the bank. Consequently, most operating forecasts for development banks are built upon the assumption that international salaries must be paid. In such cases it is hard to keep initial operating expenses down to the level of $100,000 a year. Indeed, many forecasts which we have seen have been as high as $225,000. In the case of the Ivory Coast Development Bank it was assumed that the general manager would be paid a salary of $25,000 and receive benefits of $15,000. In addition, he would be supported by an industrial

Not Official - For Illustration Only

Table 3
Proposed Colombian Bank for Cooperatives
Operating Forecast

Yr. 1 (Yr. 2-10
to be calculated)

I.   Income $37,857

  A.   Interest Earned: Loans $32,500
       (10% interest rate applied to
       average outstanding balance)

  B.   Income Earned: Deposits   0

  C.   Admission Fee (assessment against
       new members to amortize organi-
       zation expense. 5% of stock purchase
       requirement, which is 3% of new
       member's paid-in capital)   5,357

  D.   Other Income (Services, etc.)   0

II. Expenses   110,714

  A.   Interest Paid   30,000
       (1) Capital loan, AID, 6% on
           outstanding balance   30,000
       (2) Rediscounts, guarantees 6%   0

  B.   Operating Expenses   48,214
       (1) Salaries:President(GM) $7,714
           Vice Pres. and Treas.   5,142
           Secretary   5,142
           Business Analyst   3,428
           3 Secretaries   3,427
           Accountant   3,428
       (2) Other Expenses
           Directors' Expenses   142
           Travel   8,571
           Rent   1,428
           Communications   1,285
           Depreciation   142
           Supplies   3,428
           Benefits   1,142
           Meetings, Ins.,
             Contingencies   3,784

  C.   Provision for Losses on Loans   32,500

III. Net Income (Loss)   Year 1 - ($72,857)

engineer, an accountant, and an assistant. The total annual salary bill initially was forecast at over $100,000. In addition, there were the other operating expenses in this forecast of secretarial and administrative personnel directors' expenses, travel and general contingency expenses , bringing the total as mentioned above to $225,000.

As a general rule the use of local personnel should not be overlooked especially if some foreign technical assistance for an initial period can be obtained. However, it is always wise to consider in the operating forecast all the likely expenditures and costs at their normal rate. It is never a good idea in an operating forecast to anticipate the receiving of a subsidy or any technical assistance.

Even though it is to some degree and in some instances inappropriate to measure total assets by a preconceived relationship to operating expenses we can see, if we have an operating expenditure forecast of $200,000 we must acquire total assets of $20 million in order to maintain a ratio of 100:1. If we have an operating forecast expenditure of $100,000 we need total assets of $10 million.

One should always bear in mind that there is very little correlation between the total amount of capital available for lending and the number of staff personnel needed by the bank, since the size of staff depends not upon the total amount loaned but on the number of loans made in a given period of time. It may be true that the number of loans could vary with the amount of capital available, but very often the size of each loan, and hence the number of pieces into which a given amount of capital is divided, is a matter of bank policy, and can be varied by the board of directors for different reasons such as the availability of capital, the function which the bank intends to perform, the availability of projects, and many other. Staffing usually changes only with changes in the kinds of loans made and with the number of loans made. Many bankers feel that a large loan takes even less staff time than a small loan because of the business experience of large borrowers, and because of the ability of large projects to absorb the cost of technical assistance.

In summary, it may be safely stated that there is no precise way to predict the amount of capital required by a development bank, either initially or at any stage in its development. However, the approaches suggested above have been used with some success by practitioners in the field and are generally considered sound. One may use these techniques safely if one keeps in mind two important caveats:

a. <u>Optimism</u> on the part of the bank or of its organizing committee often causes them to estimate a loan volume in excess of what they can actually accomplish, and

b. <u>Inexperience</u> on the part of the bank or its organizing committee often causes them to underestimate operating costs.

PROPORTIONING OF CAPITAL BETWEEN DEBT AND EQUITY

A very important consideration with respect to capital requirements for development banks is the proportioning of capital between debt and equity. First of all, let us define both "debt" and "equity. "

"Debt" is defined as the bank total fixed payment and guarantee obligations minus those obligations of a commercial banking nature, if any, which will mature in one year, and minus also any borrowings furnished the bank in the form of subsidies (quasi equity). "Equity" is defined as all paid-in capital, surplus, free reserves, and, in addition, any borrowings as above which are furnished the bank in the form of subsidies (quasi equity).

The debt-equity ratio is used for industrial firms as well as for banks as one of the measures of financial soundness. It sets forth a certain relationship between owned and borrowed funds and is a measure both of financial risk and of investor leverage.

The essence of the dilemma of the debt-equity ratio is that equity owners, to a certain extent, would like to see a high debt-equity ratio because it gives leverage to equity capital. That is, with a high debt-equity ratio there is less risk for investors and these same investors stand to make greater profits per unit of capital invested. In addition, with a small amount of equity it is easier for a small group to maintain control. Creditors, on the other hand, are looking for the security of their investment. Although realizing that debt is an important part of the financial structure of the bank, they are interested in the security of their loan. Consequently, they hesitate to permit the borrowers to have a debt-equity ratio in excess of a certain amount.

The answer as to what is a "correct" debt-equity ratio is answerable only within a range for specific categories of economic activity. These figures may further be modified by the different business characteristics in different countries. For industries in the United States, debt-equity ratios ranging between .5 and 1.5:1 are normally accepted. For commercial banks debt-equity ratios are somewhat higher, ranging between 3 to 4:1 for smaller banks, to 9 to 12:1 for larger banks.

The reason for a difference between industry and commercial banks is because, in business, the risk of an individual industrial enterprise is much more concentrated than a commercial bank. Indeed, in industrial enterprise, fortunes may be tied up in the sale of one product. With respect to a bank, however, the risk is distributed throughout its portfolio, and its fortune may indeed depend on the business prospects of a good number of its clients.

Development banks from this standpoint should stand between industry and commercial banking. For example, the debt-equity ratio stipulated for the Small Business Investment Corporation in the United States is 4:1. Similarly, the International Finance Corporation has imposed debt-equity ratios ranging from 3 to 4:1 on the development banks in which it has invested.

In this connection it would be useful to examine the role and function of quasi equity in the capital structure of the development bank. Quasi equity represents borrowings which are furnished the development bank in the form of subsidies. The essential element which permits such debt to be counted as equity is the subordination of this debt to all other debts of the development bank and sometimes even to equity.

For example, the 75 million rupee loan which was granted in 1955 by the government of India to the Industrial Credit and Investment Corporation of India (ICICI), was subordinated both to share capital and to debt. In 1959, however, a 100 million rupee loan from the same source was subordinated only to foreign debt. Both of these are considered part of the borrowing base of the corporation. The China Development Corporation, on the other hand, has received 300 million new Taiwan dollars from the government of the Republic of China, whose debt ranks pari passu with share capital and is subordinated to all debts. Other terms and conditions under which quasi equity has been extended to development banks will be examined in detail in Sources of Capital for Development Banks. Suffice it to say for the present that this form of debt is considered by international and foreign lending agencies as part of the borrowing base.

The International Finance Corporation feels that quasi equity is an important part of the capital structure of a development bank, since it is additive to equity investment and permits a bank to start with a larger borrowing base than the bank's equity would otherwise justify. With the private industrial development banks they have sometimes recommended that quasi equity be 150 per cent of share capital. This, however, needs not to be a hard and fast rule and might be varied in other circumstances and with other kinds of development banks as the circumstances may require.

As we have mentioned above, the debt-equity ratio is a measure of financial prudence that bears a relationship to the risk that a commercial or banking institution is undergoing in the normal course of its operation. We suggest that a private industrial development bank of the stock-owning variety start off with a debt-equity ratio of 3:1 and, depending upon its prudence and success in the use of funds at this ratio, it should be permitted, after a certain period of operations, to increase this ratio to 4, 5, or 6:1.

At the present time the International Finance Corporation has permitted such successful development banks as the Pakistan Industrial Credit and Investment Corporation (PICIC), the Industrial Development Bank of Turkey (IDB/T), and the Industrial Credit and Investment Corporation of India (ICICI) to incur debt at the ratio of 4:1. When these limits are reached a development bank should give serious consideration to the issuance of additional share capital. This should be considered by all development banks before they take the step of increasing their debt-equity ratio.

Even in an inflation a development bank might be able to increase its equity capita. During inflation several years ago

in Turkey the Industrial Development Bank, although unsuc-
cessful in an effort to sell bonds, found that its stock issue
was quickly over-subscribed.

With respect to the debt-equity ratio for development
banks for cooperatives, there is good reason for this ratio to
be extremely high during the first few years of the bank's
operations. The cooperatives, which are the owners of these
banks, have always had difficulty in generating capital during
the early stages of operation. Indeed, most of the funds for
cooperative expansion have come from the earnings of the
cooperatives, rather than from investments by profit-seekers
in share capital. The reason is that the earnings of a cooperative are returned to the patrons and not to capital stockholders. Stock receives only a limited reward.

The development banks for cooperatives now being initiated in some countries in Latin America with the assistance of
AID and IDB are based on experience in capitalizing similar
banks in the United States of America. They have developed
a capitalization technique that assumes they will start off with
an extremely high debt-equity ratio. A surcharge of between
10 to 25 per cent of each interest payment (1 to 2 per cent of
the loan) is then added onto each of the borrower's interest
payments and is in fact an investment in return for which the
borrowing cooperative receives stock in the bank.

After the limits of authorized capital are reached, the
continuation of this stock purchase requirement acts in a
manner to revolve the capital of the bank by retiring the capital of those who first bought stock, and thus keeps the bank
in the hands of its current users. If at any time in the future
the bank wants to increase its equity, it merely has to sus-
pend the process by which the earliest stock is redeemed
until additional purchases by current borrowers raise paid-in
capital to the new level.

A high debt-equity ratio for development banks for cooperatives during the initial stage of their operations is also
considered to be prudent in the light of the nature of the risks
involved in cooperative lending. A cooperative bank is owned
by the cooperatives which in turn borrow its funds, and the
owner-interest acts as an additional safeguard which insures
both that the loan will be properly used and that the loan will
be repaid in due course.

SOURCES OF CAPITAL FOR DEVELOPMENT BANKS

General

Capital has been attracted to development banks from many different sources and for many different reasons. Both equity and debt capital have come from domestic public and private sources and have also come from foreign private and public sources and international sources. It will be the purpose of this section to explore in some detail the sources of capital for a development bank, both as a review and historical reckoning of sources in the past and as a guide to possible future sources.

Domestic Public Sources of Capital

A development bank, even one which intends to be privately controlled, should not overlook the possibility of local public sources for both equity and debt capital. Very often, in a developing country, the private sector is too capital-poor to provide in the beginning sufficient capital to build an adequate borrowing base. Therefore, they might turn, and indeed have turned, to local public sources for both equity and debt. It will be our purpose in this section to convey experience with local public sources of equity and debt capital and to evaluate the reason for participation on the part of both the development bank and the local public sources.

Governments of many developing countries realize that a development bank, although not a panacea, can be a very effective tool for the accomplishment of many economic and social objectives. Governments, therefore, have been sponsoring bodies either as sole owners, as participants, or as lenders, in a great number of development banks.

For example, of the 52 selected industrial development banks in Latin America which were reported in Business International,[1] 26 of these were government-owned, 5 mixed ownership, and the remaining 20 were privately owned. According to the calculations made in Table 4 the 26 government-owned development banks had assets of over $38 billion or an average of $146 million per bank. The 5 mixed banks had total assets of $632 million or $126.4 million per bank. The 20 private development banks had total assets of $114 million or $5.7 million per bank.

Table 4

Assets of Selected Industrial Development
Banks in Latin America

| Name of Bank | OWNERSHIP | | |
	Public	Private	Mixed
	(Total assets in millions of dollars)		
Argentina			
Banco Industrial de Argentina			$420
Banco Provincial de Santa Fe	$67		
Banco de la Provincia de Cordoba			82
Bolivia			
Banco Industrial		$.505	
Corporación Boliviana de Fomento	14.8		
Brazil			
Banco Nacional do Desenvolvi- mento Ecónomico	1,340		
Banco do Nordeste do Brasil	343		
Copeg Industrial Development Bank		4.1	
British Guiana			
British Guiana Credit Corporation		14.5	
Chile			
Corporación de Fomento de la Producción	282		
Colombia			
Fondo de Inversiones Privades	5.9		
Esso Investment Corporation		5	
Instituto de Fomento Industrial	4		
Corporación Financiera de Caldas		8	

Table 4, Continued

Assets of Selected Industrial Development
Banks in Latin America

Name of Bank	OWNERSHIP		
	Public	Private	Mixed
	(Total assets in millions of dollars)		
Colombia (cont'd)			
Corporación Financiera del Norte		1. 6*	
Corporación Financiera Colombiana de Desarrollo Industrial		18. 6	
Corporación Financiera Nacional		23	
Corporación Financiera del Valle		3. 9	
Costa Rica			
Banco de Costa Rica	46		
Banco Nacional de Costa Rica	55		
Corporación de Inversiones	2. 1		
Corporación Costarricense de Financiamiento Industrial			6** .9
Dominican Republic			
Corporación de Fomento Industrial	50		
El Salvador			
Instituto Salvadoreño de Fomento Industrial	6. 7		
Banco Central de Reserva	87 C217. 8		
Financiera de Desarrollo e Inversión		6. 2	
Ecuador			
Banco Nacional de Fomento	71		

Table 4, Continued

Assets of Selected Industrial Development
Banks in Latin America

Name of Bank	OWNERSHIP		
	Public	Private	Mixed
	(Total assets in millions of dollars)		

Ecuador (cont'd)

Comisión Nacional de Valores	22		

Guatemala

Instituto Nacional de Fomento de la Producción	8.6		
Financiera Guatemalteca, S.A.		1*	

Haiti

Institut de Developpement Agricole et Industriel	7		

Honduras

Banco Nacional de Fomento de Honduras	18		
Financiera Hondureña		1*	

Jamaica

Development Finance Corporation	3.9		
Small Business Loans Board	8.66		

Mexico

International, S.A.		2***	
Nacional Financiera			76.3

Nicaragua

Corporacion Nicaraguense de Inversion		2*	

Table 4, Continued

Assets of Selected Industrial Development
Banks in Latin America

| | OWNERSHIP | | |
Name of Bank	Public	Private	Mixed
Nicaragua (cont'd)			
Instituto de Fomento Nacional	19		
Panama			
Instituto de Fomento Económico	18.6		
Desarrollo Industrial, S.A.		4**	
Paraguay			
Banco Nacional de Fomento	111		
Peru			
Peruana de Fomento de Inver- siones, S.A.		6.9	
Banco Industrial del Peru			35.8
Puerto Rico			
Development Bank of Puerto Rico	122		
Surinam			
Surinam Development Bank		1*	
Uruguay			
Banco de la República Oriental del Uruguay	579.2 ℸ 9.5 billion		
Venezuela			
Creole Investment Corporation		10*	

Table 4, Continued

Assets of Selected Industrial Development
Banks in Latin America

Name of Bank	O W N E R S H I P		
	Public	Private	Mixed
Venezuela (cont'd)			
Banco Industrial de Venezuela			17.7
Corporación Financiera Venezolana de Desarrollo (Cavendez)		9	
Corporación Venezolana de Fomento	430		
	B1.9 billion		
	———	———	———
TOTAL ASSETS	$3,800	$114	$632
AVERAGE ASSETS PER BANK	$ 146.1	5.7	$126.4

* Initial paid-in capital only

** Paid-in capital stock only

*** Authorized capital only

P Pesos

B Bolivars

Source: Derived from data published by Business Interna-
        tional in August through October, 1964, as modified
        by data and information acquired at the Inter-
        American Development Bank.

One can see from this table that government support of development banking tends to be associated with significantly more capital per bank than private institutions. Indeed, this is what we would intuitively expect since a government's monetary and fiscal powers and its political position permit it to exert great influence upon the direction and mobilization of resources.

From Table 4 we might conclude that public participation in the equity of the bank will increase the likelihood that the bank will attain a significant amount of capital.

Development Bank Attitudes Toward Government Participation

At this point we might pause a moment to consider the posture of a development bank toward government participation in the ownership. Obviously, this is not a relevant consideration in the case of a publicly owned bank since the government or some other public body is the sole owner. Many private bankers, however, feel that any government participation whatsoever is an invitation to governmental control and to the injection of political and other non-economic considerations into the uses of bank funds.

Others, however, feel that government ownership can be useful even though it does carry an implied dilution of the objectives of a private business organization: the earning of a return on the investment of its stockholders.

Attitudes Toward Government Participation
in the Ownership of Development Banks

Pro	Con
1. Easier to obtain capital from many sources.	1. Political or social considerations may be brought more easily on the bank to use funds in less than optimum uses.
2. Greater possibilities of obtaining significant amounts of government capital and other government concessions.	2. The scope of the bank is likely, at government insistence from within, to be expanded with costly services.
3. Tends to lessen the threat of government expropriation or other intervention.	3. Disclosure by borrowers to a bank with government ownership will lead to "leakage" of business information to other branches of the government such as tax collection agencies.
4. "Inside track" to assist borrowers to obtain discounts, permits, concessions, and other government-controlled requirements or benefits.	4. Selection of bank personnel likely to be influenced by political favoritism at the sacrifice of capable leadership.
	5. Bank will become over-staffed with people who are not productive, yet who, because of their political connections, cannot be fired.
	6. Lack of profit motive may cause the bank to become careless with its funds.

Those organizing a development bank must be aware of the implications of government equity ownership, either directly or through a quasi-autonomous equity organization.   It is quite likely, as indicated above, that the government has motives for so doing apart from the selection of the most profitable projects, or apart from the selection of those projects which use resources in a most wise and efficient way. Most practitioners in the field of development banking recognize the absolute necessity for the development bank, if not privately owned, to be at least in some measure autonomous and free from political influence.

It must be underlined that government ownership does not always imply that political pressure will be forthcoming. Whether indeed political pressure is applied to the selection of projects depends upon the magnitude of government ownership and the kind of government ownership and the motives for government participation. If the government share is small, or if the government has purchased a class of equity which has a limitation on voting powers, or if the motives for government participation are simply to protect its investment and to keep a watchful eye on a young important development institution, in these cases government ownership need not imply political control. The private sectors of many developing countries are beginning to realize that the government can in some instances be an effective partner in development.

Reasons for Government Participation

Governments, on the other hand, have a number of reasons for their participation in both equity and debt of development banks. We might examine these reasons under the following headings:

a.   Economic Objectives

As a tool of economic development a development bank, although not a panacea, can relate to a number of pressing bottlenecks to economic growth.

(i) Entrepreneurial Development

One of the bottlenecks in the eyes of many practitioners of economic development is the critical lack of entrepreneurs. These are the individuals or, as the case may be, institutions, in a society that mobilize resources for development, and associate factors of production in productive, viable combinations to produce goods and services needed and demanded by the people.

Many writers in the field of economic development have noted the importance of the entrepreneurial function to development, and many governments, casting about for ways to accelerate the pace of growth in their countries, have turned to development banks as a way to relate to this problem. Indeed, His Majesty's Government of Nepal has invested quite heavily in the equity of the Nepal Industrial Development Corporation for one reason, among many others, because the NIDC was planning to assist entrepreneurs to take advantage of the many small industries that were potentially viable under present day conditions in Nepal.

For example, the private Industrial Credit and Investment Corporation of India (ICICI), which received in 1955, the first year of its operation, a 75 million rupee loan from the government of India, has always been extremely aware of the problem of entrepreneurial development. ICICI has made it a general policy to try to contribute to this aspect of economic development. Many projects financed by ICICI have been started by entrepreneurs for whom these projects were the first step in industry; and to quote from the statement of the Chairman of the Board, Shri G. L. Mehta, to the shareholders, on April 9, 1964:

> ICICI plays an important part in providing various ancillary services to the new entrepreneurs. We advise them on the various formalities to be fulfilled in setting up a manufacturing unit, on a suitable capital structure for the project, and on the need for and, if so, the terms of foreign collaboration arrangements.

(ii) Capital Mobilization

A development bank is a proven technique for the

mobilization of capital for productive purposes.
Most governments realize that great amounts of capital in their country, which potentially could be bent
to the use of economic development objectives, are
presently in unproductive uses, such as in land, in
buildings, luxury housing, inventories, hoards, and
especially in bank accounts or other assets in foreign
countries.

A development bank does much more for mobil-
izing capital for economic development than just the
filling out of its own capital structure. Each project that it approves has a heavy content of other
funds. And very often a development bank, with its
extensive financial contacts, both within or without a
country, can assist its borrowers in obtaining other
financing, such as suppliers' credits or investment
from other sources of capital. The Industrial Finance Corporation of India estimated in 1963 that it
had been associated since 1948 with projects whose
total investment amounted to over 30 per cent of the
private capital formation in India.

The many things that a development bank can do
to strengthen the capital market, such as underwriting, portfolio sales, stock and bond issuance,
and the like, make it an ideal tool to accomplish a
government's economic objective of capital mobilization.

(iii) Investors' Confidence

A pressing problem with which governments interested in economic growth must deal is the problem of lack of confidence on the part of domestic
and foreign investors. This lack of confidence
springs both from their lack of experience and
knowledge and, perhaps, from various kinds of instability within the country, such as political turn-
over or price changes.

Government investments in a development bank,
although certainly only one of many ways in which
the government can relate to this problem, could
be a clear demonstration of the government's

interest in economic development and its intention
to do something about it. Investors' confidence relates both to problems of entrepreneurial development and capital mobilization mentioned above, but
is separated here because of its crucial relationship to foreign capital flows.

(iv) Plan Implementation

Many countries have turned to planning as a way
of rationalizing the process by which resources are
directed to the satisfaction of consumers' needs. Although from many points of view this method of
economic development carries with it additional
problems such as fostering initiative, building confidence, and creating incentives, nevertheless planning has achieved in many countries a high degree of
respectability and will certainly be very much in use
by the developing countries until at least the "take-
off" stage of economic growth.

The relationship between formulation and plan
implementation, however, is extremely weak in
many countries. No matter how good the plan looks
on paper it somehow just doesn't get translated into
actual production. A government may look upon a
development bank as a medium through which it can
have an impact on the allocation of resources in the
country according to the development plan. Governments in many countries have chosen development banks as their chosen instruments for investment. Nacional Financiera in Mexico, Corporación
de Fomento de la Producción in Chile, and Uganda
Development Corporation, to name a few, are examples of this kind of development bank.

(v) Revenue

Another objective for the participation of a government in a development bank might be the obtaining of revenue. The investment by the Japanese
Government in the Japan Development Bank has been
extremely profitable and has yielded 6 per cent on
its borrowings and has paid to the government of
Japan more than the capital which the government

originally contributed.   In the 12-1/2 years from its establishment to September, 1963, the Japan Development Bank paid to the government of Japan $706 million (equivalent) which was composed of $339 million in interest payments and $367 million in earnings.   This is more than 8 per cent more than the bank's $650 million initial capitalization.

b.   Political and Social Objectives

Governments have invested in development banks not only to stimulate their countries' economic development but also to achieve certain political and social objectives. Governments are by nature concerned with their political position within the country and equally concerned with the attainment of certain social goals or objectives.   Consequently, there are times when it appears that their investment in development banking is oriented toward the achievement of certain of these non-economic goals, especially:

(i) Regional Balance

Very often a government is concerned with the strengths and weaknesses of particular sectors and segments of its economy and invests in a development bank in order to influence the allocation of the bank's resources to this end.   One gets the feeling that the government of Pakistan is somewhat displeased with the pattern of investments of the Pakistan Industrial Credit and Investment Corporation in that this corporation has chosen productive investments which have been overwhelmingly concentrated in West Pakistan.   Although the total amount of the loans in effect on December 21, 1963, expressed in dollars, amounted to $114.7 million, only $32.3 million had been loaned to projects located in East Pakistan, whereas almost three times that amount had been allocated to projects in Karachi and West Pakistan.   The government of Pakistan in the initial phase of PICIC financing made available 30 million rupees in October of 1957 and made another 30 million available in December of 1961.

Many observers feel that the government of

Pakistan wants PICIC to be a little more sensitive to the problem of regional balance and to increase the amount and volume of their lending in East Pakistan. It is easy to understand, on the other hand, how a private development bank such as PICIC would concentrate its lending pattern in West Pakistan. The large markets are there; infrastructure is quite a lot further advanced in West Pakistan; the existence of skilled labor, business services, and other necessary ingredients for economic development are more plentiful. East Pakistan, on the other hand, is a very low country subject to annual flooding which disrupts transportation and does not have the tradition of industrial development that West Pakistan enjoys.

The Industrial Finance Corporation of India, a development bank in which the government owns nearly half the equity, has been extremely sensitive to the geographical pattern of its investments. On Page 16 of its Annual Report for 1964 it indicates the geographical distribution of its financial assistance in considerable detail, and it points out:

> The corporation continued to give special assistance to the less developed areas of the country. A number of loans and other facilities were sanctioned during the year for industrial units to be located in less industrialized states like Assam, Andhra Pradesh, Orissa, and Uttar Pradesh.

(ii) Grass-Roots Popular Impact

No one would be naive enough to suggest that economic ills are the only cause of political strife. On the other hand, many governments realize fully well that progress in raising material standards of living is an indispensable element in political stability. Consequently, in order to satisfy public demand for economic development, many governments are casting about for institutional solutions.

A development bank has been proven to be one of the effective institutions. Through the impact made by the investment of the development bank on the economy and in the additional employment and prosperity which these investments should achieve, a government, by its investments in the development bank, is relating to this problem.

Because of the necessity for government investments somehow to reach the small investor, governments have tried interesting experiments in development banking. In India, for example, the National Small Industries Corporation lends only for capital equipment purchases by small businessmen. Pakistan, too, has a small industries corporation which provides credit to small industries in both public and private sectors, in addition to rendering technical assistance, commercial advice, and marketing advice to these industries.

Recently a local currency loan was made to the National Bank of Egypt by AID of 1 million Egyptian pounds ($2.2 million) which is earmarked specifically to provide credit for small borrowers who otherwise have no access to bank credit.

Many governments are finding that development banks for cooperatives are an ideal way in which to have grass-roots impact and at the same time make significant economic progress. A conference on the development of national markets in Latin America in October of 1964, convened by AID at the request of Dr. W.W. Rostow, braintruster of the policy planning council of the Department of State, heard many of the participants refer to cooperatives as effective instruments for achieving agricultural productivity and for rationalizing national marketing and distribution systems.

At the present time, at the request of many Latin American governments, the Inter-American Cooperative Bank Development Program, a program being administered under a contract with AID by the Fund for International Cooperative Development, is assisting local groups of cooperatives to form banks. Government support of this kind of development bank can mean real political mileage in terms of number of people affected, stimulated, and assisted.

(iii) Private Initiative

Disillusionment is growing among many of the developing countries in socialism as an engine for economic growth. Indeed, reports even from Soviet Russia indicate that profit is considered an indispensable incentive to productivity. Most people have observed that government ownership and operation of industrial enterprise abounds in inefficiency and waste, is unresponsive to consumer demand, and does not, in the absence of artificial incentives, relate effectively to the problem of industrial progress.

These governments are examining ways in which they can relate to the private sector in a way in which the advantages of private initiative can be realized within the framework of over-all government directions, and within a framework which protects people against potential abuses or excesses.

These governments are beginning now to realize that the positive incentive of personal gain, properly controlled and directed, is the only way to achieve a dynamic and viable productive economy. Their investments in development banks all over the world are eloquent testimony to this fact.

Other Domestic Public Sources of Capital

Other governmental agencies such as government-owned commercial banks, central banks, and other institutions have invested in development banks, either as instrumentalities to effect the purpose of the central government or, if they have considerable autonomy, on their own volition. It is quite likely, except possibly in the case of autonomous institutions, that the motivational patterns, although perhaps differing in emphasis, would be somewhat along the same lines as outlined above. In the case of autonomous public agencies, the fact that a development bank may be a sound investment capable of yielding a reasonable return on investment might be an additional incentive.

The investment in Industrial Finance Corporation of India

by the Reserve Bank of India, and the investment by the Central Bank of Nigeria in NIDB are examples of this kind of participation. In the latter case cited above, the Central Bank, along with the International Finance Corporation, holds its shares in trust for future private purchases.

Patterns of Domestic Public Participation

Table 5 presents certain ways in which public institutions have assisted selected development banks. The list is certainly by no means complete. Indeed, even in the cases which are described in the table, government assistance to the particular bank mentioned and to other development financing institutions in the country may be more extensive than herein described. Nevertheless, it does permit us to identify some of the typical patterns of assistance to development banks by public institutions as follows:

a.   Equity Investment

One can see from Table 5 that domestic public bodies have made a number of equity investments in development banks. In addition to the information provided in Table 5, there have been other examples of government equity purchases, such as the government of Morocco which invested in Banque Nationale pour le Developpement Economique.

Very often the government will participate as a trustee, holding equity shares against the day when they can be purchased by the private sector. Such was the case mentioned above in the investment by the Central Bank of Nigeria in the Nigerian Industrial Development Bank. Both the Central Bank of Nigeria and the International Finance Corporation picked up 24 per cent of the original stock issue apiece with the agreement that they would pari passu sell these shares in such a manner and at such a time that the private sector could purchase ownership interest in the bank without impairing its capital structure. It is anticipated that this stock will be sold gradually over a period of years.

This technique has also been suggested as a method of approach to the financing of development banks for cooperatives. The difficulty of raising equity capital for

Table 5

Some Assistance by Selected Public Institutions to Certain Development Banks

Country	Public Body	Development Bank	Form of Assist-ance	Amount* ($ equiv.)	Term (Yrs.)	Int. Rate	Grace (Yrs.)	Other
						%		
India	Government of India	Industrial Finance Corporation of India (IFC)	equity	$2.9	N.A.	N.A.	N.A.	owns approxi-mately 20%
India	Reserve Bank of India	Industrial Finance Corporation of India (IFC)	equity	2.9	N.A.	N.A.	N.A.	owns approxi-mately 20%
India	Government of India	Industrial Finance Corporation of India	loan	20	40	5	4	made in 1959
India	Government of India	Industrial Credit and Investment Corp. of India (ICICI)	loan	15	30	0	15	subordinated to share cap-ital and debt, made in 1955

India	Government of India	Industrial Credit and Investment Corporation of India (ICICI)	loan	$20	20	4-1/2	10	subordinated only to foreign debt, made in 1959
India	Government of India	Refinance Corporation for Industry	loan	55	40	4	4	made in 1958
Pakistan	Government of Pakistan	Pakistan Industrial Credit and Investment Corporation	loan	6.3	30	0	15	both loans subordinated to debt and share capital, made in 1957 and 1961 respectively
Pakistan	Government of Pakistan	Pakistan Industrial Credit and Investment Corporation	loan	6.3	40	4	4	see above

*In millions of dollars

Table 5, Continued

Country	Public Body	Development Bank	Form of Assist-ance	Amount* ($ equiv.)	Term (Yrs.)	% Int. Rate	Grace (Yrs.)	Other
Paki-stan	Government of Pakistan	Industrial Develop-ment Bank of Pakistan	loan	$6.3	30	4	4	made in 1960
Paki-stan	Government of Pakistan	Small Industries Corporation	loan	2	30	4	4	made in 1959
Ecua-dor	Government of Ecuador	National Develop-ment Bank	loan	2.9	12	3/4	4	made over a 2-yr. period, 1956–57
Ecua-dor	Government of Ecuador	Banco de Coopera-tivas del Ecuador	grant	75**				to be made over a 3-yr. period, 1965–67
Brazil	Government of Brazil	Banco Nacional do Desenvolvimento Economico	loan	14.2	35	4	4	

Bolivia	Government of Bolivia	Banco Industrial de Bolivia	loan	$300**	30	3/4	14	made in 1963
Turkey	Government of Turkey	Industrial Development Bank of Turkey	guarantee	N.A.	N.A.	N.A.	N.A.	government agreed to absorb foreign exchange risk, and in addition to guarantee a 6% dividend
Turkey	Government of Turkey	Industrial Development Bank of Turkey	Portfolio mgm't	36	N.A.	N.A.	N.A.	government turned over to IDB mgm't of 3 funds at 3% commission fee - amounts to more than 48% of total IDB resources

*In millions of dollars
**In thousands of dollars

Table 5, Continued

Country	Public Body	Development Bank	Form of Assist-ance	Amount* ($ equiv.)	Term (Yrs.)	% Int. Rate	Grace (Yrs.)	Other
China	Government of Republic	Bank of Communi-cations	loan	$875**	8	10.8	0	
China	Government of Republic of China	China Development Corporation	loan sub-ordinated to other debt, not to share capital	10	30	6	15	interest rate adjustable to provide at least a 4% spread – lent $2.5 million per yr. over 4-yr. period, 1959-63
China	Government of Republic of China	Overseas Chinese Commercial Bank	loan	250**	3	12	0	made in 1961
China	Government of Republic of China	Small Industry Loan Fund	loan	3.3	8	10.8	0	

Nigeria	Government of Nigeria	Nigerian Industrial Development Bank	loan	5. 6
Nigeria	Central Bank of Nigeria	Nigerian Industrial Development Bank	equity	1. 4

*In millions of dollars
**In thousands of dollars

such development banks from capital-poor cooperatives could possibly be overcome by equity investment on the part of a public institution with the pre-arrangement that shares would be released to cooperatives as they were able to purchase them.   Such an arrangement would lessen the clamor for loans at the door of a bank for cooperatives on opening day.   This clamor arises from many small cooperatives which have invested in the equity of the bank and which now all want a loan at the same time.

b.   Loans

One technique that has been used quite frequently and is recommended for use by the International Finance Corporation is the technique of a loan to the development bank from the public institution, usually the government, on such terms that the loan can be considered part of the borrowing base.   "Quasi equity," as this form of lending is called, has three essential characteristics.   Most important, probably, is the fact that such a loan is subordinated to all debts of the bank and usually subordinated to equity.   Its subordination to debt permits lenders to lend without fear that this quasi equity loan will constitute a prior lien on the assets of the bank. Its subordination to equity facilitates the sale of shares in the development bank.

In some cases governments which have not felt that the stock of a development bank should be thus stimulated have indicated that their loans should rank pari passu with equity and not be subordinated thereto.   Such has been the case in loans by the governments of Austria, Republic of China, and Iran to their respective development banks.

The second element of a quasi equity loan is its long-term nature, with perhaps a significant grace period.   One will note in Table 5 that the term of lending on many loans by governments to development banks is in the nature of 20, 30, to 40 years, with grace periods up to 15 years.

The third element of quasi equity is the low interest rate.   Indeed, in some instances India and Pakistan have lent at no rate of interest.   Not shown on the table is the

loan made by the government of Thailand to the Industrial
Finance Corporation of Thailand at no interest, and loans
by the government of the Philippines and the government
of Malaysia to their respective development banks at no
interest and 0.75 per cent respectively.

c.   Asset/Portfolio Transfer and Fund Administration

This technique is one which has been used to excellent advantage by governments in stimulating development banking.   As one can see from Table 5, the government of Turkey turned over to the Industrial Development Bank of Turkey the management of three funds at a
management fee of 3 per cent.   These funds originated
from U.S. capital assistance to Turkey and consisted of
the Marshall Plan Private Enterprise Fund, established
in 1951 and the Industrial Export Working Capital Fund,
established also in 1951.   As pointed out above, total
resources provided by these three funds amount to over
48 per cent of the total resources of funds available to
the bank for lending.

Not shown on Table 5 is the transfer by the government of Iran of the portfolio of the Industrial Credit
Bank of Iran to the private Industrial Mining and Development Bank of Iran.   Also, the government of
Ethiopia transferred the portfolio of the Agriculture and
Commercial Bank to the Development Bank of Ethiopia;
and the government of Japan transferred the equivalent
of $237 million to the Japan Development Bank, which
comprised the entire portfolio of the Reconversion
Finance Bank of Japan.

d.   Guarantees and Agreements

Table 5 indicates that a number of governments
have supported development banking by making certain
advantageous agreements with the development bank. For
two loans, for example, the government of Turkey
agreed to absorb the foreign exchange risk by guaranteeing to convert into dollars local currency repayments of
borrowers on loans made by the bank in foreign exchange.   In addition the government agreed to guarantee
a 6 per cent dividend on the stock of the bank such dividend, if and when paid by the government, was to

operate as a loan to the development bank. In practice this contingent commitment was very little used by the bank except in the very early stages of its operation.

The government of Pakistan absorbed the maintenance of value risk on the first World Bank loan to the Pakistan Industrial Credit and Investment Corporation. Since then, however, it has not so guaranteed loans made to PICIC.

In Latin America several governments have been willing to undertake the maintenance of value burden by prearrangement with development banks. The government of Colombia, for example, is requiring the Instituto Colombiano de Reforma Agraria (INCORA) to repay only the amount of currency borrowed. The Colombian Government is also taking the foreign exchange risk in the case of a dollar credit to the Instituto de Credito Agropecuario. In Ecuador, too, the government seems willing to assume part or all of the risk of maintenance of value for certain kinds of development banks.

Other kinds of agreements that the government might make with a development bank very often will not lead to actual cash outflow on the part of the government but merely serve to underscore and undergird the confidence which the government has in the potential of the institution. Such was the case in which the government of India guaranteed IFC's payment of both principal and a minimum annual dividend of 2.25 per cent on the first series of shares and 4 per cent on the second series of shares. In actual practice, however, the earnings of the Industrial Finance Corporation have been sufficiently high so that this guarantee was only used in the beginning of operations of the bank.

e.   Discounting Facilities

The provision of discounting facilities to development banks by governments is similar to a loan. The liquidity of a bank is enhanced if it can sell the assets it acquired to another institution in order to obtain funds to relend. The ability to sell or discount its assets to another institution and thus obtain additional funds is extremely important to a development bank specially in view of the fact that it is designed to provide medium-and long-term loans.

The government of Colombia has extended discounting facilities to several of the Colombian Development Banks with an interest spread of 5 per cent per year with maturities up to five years. The banks, however, remain liable for obligations which are discounted.

Domestic Private Sources of Capital

The ability of a development bank to raise equity or debt locally depends on a number of factors including among them:

a.   The availability and sources of such funds.

b.   The confidence of the public in the quality and caliber of the people chosen to manage the bank.

c.   The leverage of equity capital or the security for debt.

d.   If the bank has been operating for some time, the soundness of its operations and its likely prospects of future success.

e.   Likely future price conditions will determine the choice between debt and equity. In an inflation, unless the debt is linked to something whose real value is maintained, an investor, if he invests at all, will prefer equity.

f.   The terms and conditions under which the proposed investment is offered to the proposed investor.

In addition to these considerations, there are a number of things that may be said about domestic private sources of capital for development banks. Some of the most significant private sources are as follows:

a.   Commercial banks
b.   Insurance companies
c.   Business corporations
d.   Cooperatives
e.   Private individuals

In general the reasons for private investment in development banks are the same in developing countries as they are anywhere. Investors usually seek to move in their investment portfolio toward one or two of three possible financial objectives:

    a.   Present income
    b.   Future growth
    c.   Security of investment

From the standpoint of earnings, a development bank cannot hope to compete with many profit opportunities in developing countries in the short run because of the many obstacles and hurdles that are inherent in initial start-up and operation of a development bank. For the first two or three years, in the absence of any subsidy from the government or any other sources, a development bank is quite likely to lose money until its loan volume is sufficient to pay for the administrative costs. The Banco de Cooperativas del Ecuador was able to project in the black from the very beginning only because of a three-year grant by the Agency for International Development and because of a subsidy from the government of Ecuador.

After a few years of operation, however, the earnings potential of a development bank should be very good and in the long run the earnings should be even better, provided that the development bank choses its investments wisely and doesn't let administrative costs get out of hand. The Industrial Development Bank of Turkey, for example, during the last decade has been paying a dividend of the legal maximum of 12 per cent each year and still building up sizable reserves.

From the standpoint of growth, an equity investment in a development bank is likely to be a very sound investment. Development banks will grow probably as fast as, or faster than, the rest of the economy, depending, of course, on the productivity of the uses made of its funds. If the bank has the authority to make equity investments (and it usually does), these investments, if wisely chosen, will through capital gains and payment of dividends enhance both the earning capacity of the bank and the saleability of its own obligations.

During an inflation equity investments in a development

bank are much more easily sold than debt in the absence of any arrangement tying the debt to the level of prices. As we have noted, the Development Bank of Turkey, during inflation, had trouble selling its bonds but over-subscribed its stock. One would naturally expect that a debt instrument with its fixed income and repayment obligations would be less attractive during a time of rising prices than would be a share of ownership or equity in a development bank. A share of ownership would be presumed to rise in price along with the other prices in the economy.

From the standpoint of security, a development bank is also a good investment. The diversity of its portfolio makes an investment in a development bank a less risky thing than an investment in a corporation. Under some circumstances the shares of a development bank will be able to be traded even in countries where the capital market is not very well articulated. Most people feel that development banks will play an important role in their countries' economic growth. Therefore, they tend to feel that investment in a development bank is reasonably secure.

Let us now examine certain subsectors of the domestic private sector which have invested in development banks together with some of the reasons.

Commercial Banks and Other Financial Institutions

Commercial banks have in the past lent significant support to the formation of development banks both in the purchase of equity and in some cases consortia to provide debt.

For example, a consortium of banks in Finland provided a line of credit of $8 million to the Industrialization Fund Corporation in Finland. Among the main shareholders of this bank are three private Finnish commercial banks, in addition to the Central Bank of Savings Banks, the Central Bank of Cooperative Societies, and the Postal Savings Bank. The China Development Corporation, too, was established by, among others, leading bankers in Taiwan. Development banks in Thailand, Philippines, India, Pakistan, Turkey, Ivory Coast, Colombia, Venezuela, and many other countries have obtained equity capital from commercial banks and other financial domestic private institutions.

As we pointed out above, the reasons for their participation are partly because in their judgment an investment in
a development bank offers the probability of future earnings,
offers the prospect of excellent growth, and offers the security of a diverse portfolio. In addition, however, there are
other reasons why such institutions can be induced to participate in the formation or strengthening of a development
bank. Some of the most important of these reasons are as
follows:

a. Increased Deposits

A commercial bank, of course, depends for its
sources of capital mainly upon demand and time deposits
which are placed there by individuals in anticipation of
immediate or possible future need. Businesses are
prime users of the deposit facilities of commercial banks
and it is the knowledge of this fact that encourages a
commercial bank to assume an ownership interest in a
development bank. Development banks are usually not
banks of deposits and therefore do not compete with a
commercial bank for sources of funds. Development
banks in turn usually meet the immediate and long-term
lending requirements and again do not compete with the
short-term loans that are made by commercial banks.
Commercial banks feel that their participation in the
equity of a development bank may strengthen their position in the business community of a country, which will
indirectly result in increased deposits and use of their
services and facilities by both the bank and the bank's
borrowers.

b. More Business

A commercial bank may make an investment in a
development bank to gain an entry to the business community which will result in joint financing of profitable
business projects. As pointed out above, commercial
banks do not feel competition with development banks
for the uses of their funds. Situations might arise in
which the development bank would be providing the long-
term fund, with the commercial bank providing the
short-term debt capital.

c.   Image

Related to the above is the image which a commercial bank is projecting in a particular economy. Generally speaking its clients are businessmen and individuals
who come to the commercial bank because it can provide
them with financial services. A commercial bank, therefore, would try to project an image of competence and
broad financial contact within the domestic community.
An investment in the equity of a development bank would
be one important part of this image.

d.   Contacts

In its rendering of financial services to clients, a
commercial bank is often in a position of advising on the
total financial structure of a project. The contacts which
a commercial bank would make as a result of its investment in a development bank with international sources of
capital, with international agencies, and with other elements of the domestic foreign financial community should
be valuable to the commercial bank for the rendering of
this kind of service.

e.   Other

There is a general feeling that a development bank is
an integral part of an economic development program
and the commercial bank is probably proud from a patri-
otic point of view to participate in the economic development of its country.

Sometimes there may be pressure exerted directly
or indirectly on the commercial banks by the government,
which helps to induce them through fear or favor to make
an investment in a development bank. Another possible
minor reason applicable only in special instances is the
desire of the commercial bank to do through a development bank what it is not permitted to do itself. Commercial banks in Mexico, for example, initiated
financieras and made investments through them on terms
which would not be possible for them to make directly.
In the early 1950's, however, the government of Mexico
stepped in to regulate these financieras in the same manner as the commercial banks so that the advantage gained

was only temporary. U. S. commercial banks have
set-up investment corporations under the Edge Act to
comply with laws prohibiting a commercial bank from
taking equity positions.

Insurance Companies

Insurance companies are also interested in investments
in development banks for their potential earnings, for their
prospects of future growth, and for the security of a diversified portfolio. The growth possibility is probably the most attractive to insurance companies. An insurance company,
when it insures an individual, undertakes a commitment that
is not likely to be realized until some future date is reached.
This fact requires that an insurance company make the kind of
investments with these funds that will insure their maintenance of value until the time that they are called upon for use.

Insurance companies in many countries have realized
that an investment in the equity of a development bank is an
excellent way in which to insure that its investment will grow
and keep pace with the economy. The law in many countries
is designed to prevent capital flight of the liquid assets of
insurance companies and in Mexico, for instance, insurance
companies are required to reinvest their liquid assets in that
country. Thus, an investment in a development bank either
in equity or in debt might appeal to insurance companies if
properly presented to them.

One must not forget that as insurers of the population,
insurance companies have a financial interest in general
well-being and would be doing themselves an indirect favor if
by their investments the material well-being of the population
could be improved. In addition, it does the local image of an
insurance company no damage to be associated with such a
popular locally owned institution as a development bank.
A goodly number of development banks have obtained either
equity or debt financing from insurance companies. A few
such banks are as follows:

Austrian Credit and Investment Corporation
Industrial Finance Corporation of Thailand
Industrial Credit and Investment Corporation of India
Pakistan Industrial Credit and Investment Corporation

Banque Nationale pour le Development Economique
in Morocco.

Business Corporations, Cooperatives, and Individuals

Many businesses in developing countries have realized
that although development banking may be quite alien to their
customary economic endeavors, investment may be beneficial
to the corporation for a number of reasons.

Again, as above, it may offer profit to the investor in
the form of earnings, growth, or security, since each bank
is different as we pointed out above and the opportunity for
profit must be evaluated by the investor in each case. In
addition to potential profits, however, many business corporations are well-advised to consider equity or debt investment in a development bank on the grounds that the bank may
some day be a source of funds for that business. Although
such a business should never attempt to influence the making
of a loan by a bank, it is reasonable to suspect that other
things being equal it would receive prior consideration for
financial services as compared with an applicant who had no
financial interest in the bank.

As a source of information, investment in a development
bank is also valuable for a business corporation. It has an
inside track to many business opportunities which it can explore with the applicant on its own or even sometimes at the
request of the bank. Many excellent joint ventures have been
thus worked out between applicants of the bank and investors
in a bank.

As above, investment in such a popular development institution as a development bank does the company's public
image no harm. In many countries, indeed, corporations
with a heavy dose of foreign financial control are quite anx-
ious to improve their image in a country. Not only does it
help sell their product but it, indeed, also paves the way
with governments for more equitable treatment as compared
with all domestically owned corporations. One of the most
pressing problems that many corporations have identified in
these countries is that of convincing the government that they
are sincerely interested in the development of the country
and not just in their own profits.

Cooperative organizations, too, have invested in development banks. Recently, seeking to strengthen the cooperative financing system in Latin America, the Agency for International Cooperative Development contracted with the Fund for International Cooperative Development, a private organization, to undertake the task of assisting Latin American cooperatives to set up development banks in countries where they appear to be needed and appropriate. The entire amount of equity capital in most cases has come from the cooperatives themselves.

Equity is gradually acquired by a development bank for cooperatives by adding a surcharge of a certain per cent to each interest payment, such surcharge being used to purchase stock in the bank in the name of the borrowing cooperative. When the limits of authorized capital are reached, additional stock purchases then retire capital stock on a first-in-first-out basis, thus assuring that the bank is always owned by its current users.

Many different kinds of cooperatives have invested in cooperative banks. The principal investors in Banco de Cooperativas del Ecuador have been credit unions which see the bank as a source of funds. The cooperative bank permits certain qualified credit unions to borrow up to three times their members' savings. This gives the credit union movement additional leverage since unions can hold out the prospect that one sucre saved commands three sucres in borrowing power.

Individuals, too, have invested in development banks. The development banks which have issued public share offerings have experienced, in many cases, excellent success. As mentioned above, the Industrial Development Bank of Turkey, when frustrated in its attempt to sell bonds during an inflationary period, found that its equity share offering was oversubscribed within a short time.

The Cyprus Development Corporation (CDC) offers a good example, too, of how a properly organized and publicized development bank can excite and arouse a high degree of local interest. The board of directors of CDC decided to offer initially 400,000 shares and on June 14, 1963, they appointed eight banks as local agents. A small brokerage firm agreed to act as agent abroad, mostly in the United Kingdom.

By June 27, 1963, the prospectus was officially published in local newspapers. A television program was written and produced in both the Greek and Turkish languages. A simple question and answer booklet was printed to be available at all bank branches along with the prospectus and application forms. On July 1, the subscription lists were opened in Cyprus and London and by July 11, it was apparent that the issue would be over-subscribed. The directors of the bank decided to close the subscription lists as of July 20. By July 20, the issue had, indeed, been over-subscribed by more than 100 per cent (803,269 shares). The success of a public share offering will depend in great measure on the amount of publicity and pre-sale preparation which is done by the bank. It is extremely important that the timing of the advertisements, the notices, the prospectus, and the applications be perfectly coordinated. Development banks in Venezuela, Colombia, Morocco, and Philippines, to name a few, have also had excellent success in public share offerings.

Foreign Public and International Sources

General

Since the first World Bank loans to the Industrial Development Bank of Turkey and the Development Bank of Ethiopia, foreign public and international lending through development banks has been a popular method of foreign aid. It has been estimated by the author that very close to $2 billion has been channeled to private agricultural and industrial efforts through development banks all over the world from foreign public and international sources. The principal sources of funds for this relending have been the following:

a.   Agency for International Development
b.   International Bank for Reconstruction and
       Development
c.   International Finance Corporation
d.   International Development Association
e.   Inter-American Development Bank
f.   Export-Import Bank of Washington

One of the principal reasons for the popularity of lending to private industrial and agricultural projects to development banks is that these banks have proven the ability to reach the small investor or small farmer. They are familiar with local conditions, laws, economic and political situations and can do a much better job of supervising the loan.

In considering the ways in which development banks of today can obtain the financing they need to grow, the solicitation of debt and equity from foreign public and international sources appears to be one of the most useful channels. It therefore behooves us to explore each one of these in turn, to observe their past pattern of lending both geographically and functionally and to explore briefly some of the touchstones which are liable, if pressed, to release funds to a development bank.

IBRD, IFC, AND IDA

The World Bank family has been an important source of lending to development banks. The International Bank for Reconstruction and Development which is popularly known as the World Bank is the mother institution of this family and is supported by its 103 member nations. Principally, it extends hard currency loans to development banks and through June 30, 1964, had extended $405.6 million to private borrowers through industrial development banks.

The International Finance Corporation and the International Development Association, both offshoots and close affiliates of the World Bank, were organized by members of the bank in 1956 and 1960 respectively. The IFC has been a partner with the World Bank in the Building of seven private development finance companies since September, 1961, when its charter was amended to permit it to take equity positions. The International Development Association (IDA) gives the World Bank flexibility to invest in countries with balance of payments problems. The terms and conditions of loans to the development bank itself are not significantly different from World Bank terms and can be considered the same for all practical purposes.

As one can see from Table 6, the World Bank had made 29 hard currency loans to eleven private development banks. Its average loan is about $10 million. The present interest rate being charged by the bank is 5.5 per cent per annum, but the bank agrees with the borrower that the rate charged the borrower will be the current World Bank rate when each development bank sub-loan is made. The terms of World Bank

Table 6
World Bank, IFC, IDA
Financial Assistance to Private Industrial Development Finance Companies to October 31, 1965

Country and Institution	IBRD No. Loans	Total IBRD (mil. $)	Int. Range (%)	Term Range (Yrs.)	IDA Loan (mil. $)	Int. IDA (%)	Term IDA (Yrs.)	IFC (mil. $)	Term IFC
Austria									
Oesterreichische Investitionskredit AG (IVK)	3	23.3	5-1/2*	10-15					
China									
China Development Corporation (CDC)	1	15.0	5-1/2	15	5	Variable, currently 9.84%	30		
Colombia									
Corporación Financiera Colombiana (CFC Bogota)								2.0	Equity
Corporación Financiera de Caldas (CFC Caldas)								0.7	Equity

*The interest rate will be the current World Bank rate when each development finance company sub-loan is made.

Table 6, Continued

Country and Institution	IBRD No. Loans	Total IBRD (mil.$)	Int. Range (%)	Term Range (Yrs.)	IDA Loan (mil.$)	Int. IDA (%)	Term IDA (Yrs.)	IFC (mil.$)	Term IFC
Colombia (cont'd)									
Corporacion Financiera del Norte (CFN)								2.0	Equity
Ethiopia									
Development Bank of Ethiopia (DBE)	2	4.0	4-5-1/2*	10-20					
Finland									
Industrialization Fund (IFF)	2	21.0	5-1/2*	15					
India									
Industrial Credit and Investment Corporation of India (ICICI)	6	139.9	4-5/8 to 5-1/2*	7-15				0.2	Equity

Iran Industrial and Mining Development Bank of Iran (IMDBI)	2	15.2	5-1/2*	15
Israel Industrial Development Bank of Israel (IDBI)	1	20.0	5-1/2	15
Ivory Coast Banque Ivoirienne de Developpement Industrial (BIDI)	0.2	Equity		
Liberia Liberian Bank for Indus- trial Development and Investment (LBIDI)	0.3	Equity		

*The interest rate will be the current World Bank rate when each development finance company sub-loan is made.

105

Table 6, Continued

Country and Institution	IBRD No. Loans	Total IBRD (mil.$)	Int. Range (%)	Term Range (Yrs.)	IDA Loan (mil.$)	Int. IDA (%)	Term IDA (Yrs.)	IFC (mil.$)	Term IFC
Malaysia									
Malaysian Industrial Development Finance Ltd. (MIDFL)	1	8.0	5-1/2*	15				0.8	Equity
Morocco									
Banque Nationale pour le Developpement Economique (BNDE)	1	15.0	5-1/2*	15				1.5	Equity
Nigeria									
Nigerian Industrial Development Bank Ltd. (NIDB)		109.1		7-15				1.4	Equity
Pakistan									
Pakistan Industrial Credit and Investment Corporation Ltd. (PICIC)	6	109.1	5-3/4 to 5-1/2*	7-15				0.4	Equity

	No.	Interest Rate (%)	Term (years)	Amount ($M)	Equity ($M)	
Philippines						
Private Development Corporation of the Philippines (PDCP)	1	5-1/2*	15	15.0	0.4	Equity
Spain						
Banco del Desarrollo Economico Espanol (BANDESCOO)					0.6	Equity
Thailand						
Industrial Finance Corporation of Thailand (IFCT)	1	5-1/2*	15	2.5	0.2	Equity
Turkey						
Turkiye Sinai Kalkinma Bankasi A.S. (TSKB)	2	3-3/4 to 4-7/8	15	17.6	0.9	Equity
		5-1/2	20	15		
Venezuela						
C.A. Venezolana de Desarrollo (CAVENDES)					1.3	Equity
	25			405.6	12.8	

---

*The interest rate will be the current World Bank rate when each development finance company sub-loan is made.

loans to development banks generally run around 15 years. Repayment generally starts two or three years after the signing of the loan agreement.

The geographical pattern of lending has seen the overwhelming majority of World Bank family loans and investments go to the Near East South Asia (NESA) region. Of the $443.4 million that the World Bank family has committed almost $325 million has gone to NESA. Of that $325 million $250 million has been committed to two banks - one in India (ICICI) and one in Pakistan (PICIC). The Far East ranks second in the geographical pattern with $47 million, principally because of a $15 million loan to the Private Development Corporation (PDC) of the Philippines. Europe ranks third in the geographical pattern of World Bank lending with $45 million. Africa is next with $22.4 million and Latin America last with $4.2 million.

The International Finance Corporation invested in 13 private development banks up to June 30, 1964. Its average investment in each bank was around $1 million and it is usually the catalyst that has in the past brought the various equity participants of a bank together.

One can see from Table 6 that the World Bank's financial assistance to development banks extends only to private industrial finance companies. By a policy determination the IBRD restricts its lending to development banks to those which are privately controlled in spite of the loan made in 1950 to the Development Bank of Ethiopia. The IFC, on the other hand, is constrained by its charter to limit its investments to private enterprise. However, some World Bank projects loans have been channeled into specific agricultural projects through government development banks. For example, $25 million has been extended recently to Corporacion de Fomento de la Produccion (CORFO) in Chile for such purpose.

But the experience of the World Bank and the IFC over the past years is that development finance companies are most likely to be successful if their ownership is predominantly private. They feel that private ownership is the best way to assure sound investment policies and to assure the retention of experienced management. They feel that operations of the bank should be conducted along sound business lines and by strict adherence to economic rather than political criteria.

The IFC prefers that a development bank should be regarded as genuinely national: That is, a majority of its stock should be owned within the country. As a matter of policy, the IFC regards itself as an institution which partakes of the national character of the country in which it is investing. As mentioned before in another connection, IFC purchased 24. 5 per cent of the equity in the Nigerian Industrial Development Bank, with an agreement to sell this stock at some later time to investors in Nigeria.

The IFC also prefers that private development banks should be as broadly owned as possible and not controlled by a single investor or small group of investors. They feel that such a representative pattern of ownership permits the government of that country to recognize that the successful operation of the bank is not merely in the interest of a few but in the public interest. With respect to government ownership, the IFC has, in the Nigerian case, participated with the government in an investment in a development bank, after being assured that the NIDB was effectively isolated from governmental control, and that the government was prepared to sell its shares to domestic private investors, at some future time.

Even though all the above ingredients are present, IFC may still be reluctant to participate in the formation of a development bank or in the strengthening of an existing bank, if it is not convinced that three additional conditions exist:

a. The development and strengthening of the private sector must be consistent with the nation's over-all aims and objectives. IFC points out that it would be pointless to establish a development bank in a country whose objective was social ownership and control of production.

b. The country must have an adequate absorptive capacity for the type of financial assistance which the development bank is designed to provide. IFC feels that in order for a development bank to be successful in a country, it must possess a nucleus of entrepreneurial and managerial talent, a reasonably broad market for the products of new enterprises, some natural resources, and some infrastructure. IFC feels that if there is not a fairly large volume of private industrial activity which could utilize funds if made available to them through a development bank at a certain minimum volume, a development bank could not be viable.

This is an excellent word of caution to those who feel that development banks are in some way conditions precedent to private industrial development. Some people have criticized this policy as being too coldly businesslike and feel that the International Finance Corporation should be more responsive to long-run development objectives. Critics point out that private business will never gain a foothold in a country unless it is accompanied from the start by the very kind of financial and technical assistance that a development bank is designed to provide. Therefore, one has seen development banks spring up throughout the world mostly without IFC assistance, as a reflection of the conviction that development finance must be a condition concurrent to private industrial growth and not a condition subsequent.

c. The third condition is that IFC needs to be convinced that the financial function of the proposed development bank is, indeed, filling a clearly defined gap in the capital market. They point out that if financial assistance of the kind which the development bank is likely to offer is already available from existing sources, no purpose is served by its establishment. On the other hand, IFC officials are quick to point out that there are few suppliers of medium- and long-term capital in the new nations. This condition is very easily satisfied in most instances.

As pointed out above, once the World Bank group is convinced that a development finance company is feasible or that an existing development finance company needs strengthening, they are qualified to give assistance far beyond that of providing capital. Their assistance can include help in drafting the articles of association of the bank, giving advice on appropriate operating policies, identifying top management, and in serving as a catalyst to bring other sponsors together. IFC has responded to requests of other sponsors to nominate a member to the board of directors of the development

bank in which IFC is investing if in their own judgment
such membership can be a constructive influence in the
company's affairs.   In their opinion the lack of skill and
experience on the part of the staff of a new development
bank causes project appraisal to be the bank's greatest
weakness, and they feel that the selection of sound projects is probably the most important task of the bank officials.   Very often project appraisals are referred to
the bank or IFC for advisory opinions, even when such
submission is not necessary.

Development banks borrowing from the World Bank group
should keep in mind that procurement of goods and services may be from any country which is a member of the
World Bank group, including Switzerland, which is not
a member but which has been a great source of funds to
the World Bank.

Inter-American Development Bank

The Inter-American Development Bank, or "El BID" as
it is called by the Latin Americans, made available over
$276 million (equivalent) to private agricultural and industrial
projects through development banks (private, public, and
mixed) from 1961-65. A large part, $103 million, was speci-
fically earmarked for agricultural relending; $129 million
was specifically earmarked for industrial relending; $73
million had no specification tied to it, presuming that the funds
would be re-lent both for qualified industrial and agricultural
projects; $11 million was made available to cooperatives in
Chile and Costa Rica. The average loan made by BID to intermediate credit institutions is about $5.7 million, but the 51
loans listed in Table 7 were received by 35 institutions, so
that the average amount per institution would be slightly
greater ($8.1 million).

Development banks have tapped both of the principal
funds of the bank, the Fund for Ordinary Operations from
which funds are available generally at 6 per cent interest and
the Fund for Special Operations from which the interest rate
is around 4 per cent. BID requires that the loans be repaid
in currency lent which makes them hard currency loans, but
very often, as one can see from the table, local currencies
or third-country currencies are made available to qualified
borrowers.

Table 7

Inter-American Development Bank Global Loans to Intermediate Credit Institutions
for Relending to the Private Sector

Development Bank	Amount* (Gross of Participations)	Date	% Interest Rate	Term (Yrs.)	Grace (Yrs.)
Argentina					
1. Banco de la Nación 12.5 million in dollars 7.5 million in pesos 5 million in lire	25	4-63	5-3/4	15	3
2. Banco de la Nación 6 million in dollars 6 million in DM 3 million in pesos	15	12-64	6	15	2
3. Consorcio de Bancos Provinciales 14 million in dollars 1 million in pesos	15	8-61	5-3/4	12	4
Bolivia					
4. Corporación Boliviana de Fomento	10	2-61	4-1/2	13	3

Brazil					
5. BNDE 12 million in dollars 15 million in cruzeiros	27	7-64	5-3/4	15	3
6. Banco do Nordeste do Brasil	10	4-61	4-1/2	15	4
7. Caixa Economica do Estado do Minas Gerais	6.4	4-62	1-1/4	11	1
8. Banco de Credito Agricola do Espírito Santo	2	1-63	1-1/4	20	1
Chile					
9. CORFO 4.5 million in dollars 1.5 million in escudos	6	4-61	5-3/4	12	3
10. CORFO	6	3-64	5-3/4	12	3
11. CORFO and CORA	10	12-61	1-1/4	11	1

*In millions of dollars

Table 7, Continued

Development Bank	Amount* (Gross of Participations)	Date	% Interest Rate	Term (Yrs.)	Grace (Yrs.)
Colombia					
12. Corporación Financiera Colombiana de Desarrollo Industrial	1.05	4-61	5-3/5	10	2
.5 million in dollars					
8.5 million in pesos					
13. Banco de la República	3	10-63	5-3/4	12-1/2	2-1/2
14. Fondo de Desarrollo do Zonas Cafeteras y Federación Nacional de Cafeteros	7	5-64	1-3/4	20	1
Costa Rica					
15. Banco Nacional	3	11-61	5-3/4	12	3
2.5 million in dollars					
.5 million in colones					
16. Banco Nacional	1	4-63	4	21	2.5

	*				
Costa Rica (cont'd)					
17. Banco de Costa Rica	3	8-62	5-3/4	12	3
2.5 million in dollars					
.4 million in colones					
Dominican Republic					
18. Banco Agrícola	6	10-63	5-3/4	12	3
4.5 million in dollars					
1.5 million in escudos					
19. Banco Agrícola	3	8-63	1-3/4	11	1
Ecuador					
20. Comisión Nacional de Valores	2.3	8-61	5-3/4	12	2
1.6 million in dollars					
.7 million in sucres					
21. Comisión Nacional de Valores	2.3	7-61	5	14	3
2 million in dollars					
.3 million in sucres					

*In millions of dollars

Table 7., Continued

Development Bank	Amount* (Gross of Participations)	Date	% Interest Rate	Term (Yrs.)	Grace (Yrs.)
Ecuador (cont'd)					
22. Banco Nacional de Fomento	.097	7-62	4	4	2
23. Sistema de Crédito de Fomento	6	10-62	4	14	4
El Salvador					
24. Banco Central de Reserva	2.5	8-61	5-3/4	13	3
25. Banco Central de Reserva	2	8-61	1-3/4	11	1
Guatemala					
26. Banco de Guatemala	5	8-61	5-3/4	12	2
4.2 million in dollars					
.8 in quetzales					
Haiti					
27. Banque Nationale de la Republique d'Haiti	3.5	4-61	4	15	3
Honduras					
28. Banco Nacional de Fomento	6	4-62	4	16	4

29.	Banco Nacional de Fomento	2.5	8-62	1-3/4	21	1
Mexico						
30.	Nacional Financiera 2 million in dollars 1 million in pesos	3	8-61	5-3/4	10	2
31.	Nacional Financiera	5.7	11-61	5-3/4	20	3
Nicaragua						
32.	Instituto de Fomento Nacional	2	3-61	5-3/4	12	2
33.	Instituto de Fomento Nacional	2.3	7-64	5-3/4	15	3
34.	Banco Nacional de Nicaragua	4.5	12-64	4	15	
Panama						
35.	Banco Nacional	1	12-64	4	14	3
36.	Instituto de Fomento Económico	2.9	12-61	4	16	4

*In millions of dollars

Table 7, Continued

Development Bank	Amount* (Gross of Participations)	Date	% Interest Rate	Term (Yrs.)	Grace (Yrs.)
Paraguay					
37. Banco Nacional de Fomento 3.5 million in dollars .5 million in guaranies	4	7-64	4	15	3
38. Banco Nacional de Fomento	3	3-61	5-3/4	10	3
39. Banco Nacional de Fomento	2.9	12-62	1-3/4	21	1
Peru					
40. PERUINVEST	.75	11-63	5-3/4	12	2
41. Banco Industrial del Perú	2.5	10-62	5-3/4	12	2
42. Banco Industrial del Perú	5	12-63	5-3/4	12	2
Uruguay					
43. Banco de la República Oriental	5	12-63	5-3/4	12-1/2	3-1/2

Venezuela					
44. Banco Agrícola y Pecuario 4.9 million in dollars 1.1 million in pesos	6	4-63	5-3/4	10	2
45. Corporación Venezolana de Fomento 7 million in dollars 3 million in bolivares	10	5-61	5-3/4	12	2
46. Corporación Venezolana de Fomento	10	11-64	6	12	2
Central America Regional					
47. CABEI 5 million in dollars 1 million in various	6	4-63	4	20	3

*In millions of dollars

Table 7, Continued

Development Bank	Amount* (Gross of Participations)	Date	% Interest Rate	Term (Yrs.)	Grace (Yrs.)
Central America Regional (cont'd)					
48. CABEI 7.8 million in dollars .4 million in various	8.2	12-64	4	20	3
TOTAL LOANS	278.5				
Average Amount per Loan	5.7				
Average Loan per Institution	8.1				

*In millions of dollars

To be eligible for a loan from BID, the development bank must be located in one of the countries belonging to the Organization of American States (OAS), which includes all of the Latin American republics except Cuba. The loans made by BID to intermediate credit institutions are between 12 and 20 years with two to three years' grace, although there have been some few exceptions.

As compared with the World Bank, a relatively large part of the BID funds have been channeled through development banks. The explanation seems to be that because of the newness of the institution and because it takes time to build up staff capability, BID in the beginning has felt it necessary to rely extensively upon the loan analysis and project evaluation capability of its development bank borrowers. In addition, BID officials realize the other advantages to development banks: their ability to reach smaller projects, their ability to evaluate more carefully background economic and political conditions which may affect the borrower, their ability to relate to and identify with the borrower and, consequently, service him better, and many other advantages.

To be eligible for a BID loan, the development bank must be an integral part of the national banking and financing system of the particular country concerned, and it must be in some manner under the supervision of the government agency responsible for the country's credit activities. In contradistinction to the World Bank policy of lending only to private institutions, the financing institutions eligible for BID loans can be public, private, or mixed and can operate at the national, provincial, or international level, but the ultimate beneficiaries must be small- and medium-scaled private business, in any sector related to economic development.

In order to arrive at a judgment with respect to the eligibility of a bank for a BID loan, BID will investigate the institution's legal framework, administration, financial structure, operating policies, operating expenses, if any, technical and human resources, and the economic and social results that have been achieved since its establishment.

BID also offers technical assistance covering many different areas, such as operating policies, administrative structures, mobilization of resources, accounting and auditing systems, training of personnel, and other specific aid on an ad hoc basis.

As one can see from Appendix A, BID requires a rather detailed volume of information from a prospective borrowing development bank before it will consider an intensive review of the loan application.

In some cases, especially in countries whose national development plans have not yet been approved at the time the particular development bank is negotiating its loan with BID, BID very often finds it necessary to agree on the kinds of projects that will be financed with the loan. Among the restrictions sometimes imposed, the following may be mentioned:

a. Operations that are merely the refinancing and refunding of earlier debts or the substitution of one creditor by another.

b. Production for export of goods of which there is already world overproduction.

c. Production of luxury items for domestic consumption.

d. Direct financing of working capital.

e. Purchase or lease of land even for the location of enterprises that are receiving financing.

f. Operations for the marketing of products for the purpose of price stabilization.

A guarantee is usually required by BID on loans that it makes to development banks and this guarantee is usually issued by the nation in which the bank is located on terms and conditions agreed upon by BID. In some instances a guarantee has been accepted on the part of the central bank acting as such or as fiscal agent of the government. In addition to general guarantees mentioned above, in certain cases specific guarantees are agreed upon. In such cases the development bank has provided BID with promissory notes of various sub-borrowers payable to BID. This collateral is maintained during the life of the loan in an amount equivalent to at least 120 per cent of the balance owed by the bank to BID.

BID, when it lends, does not make available a volume of funds to be indiscriminately incorporated with any other funds a development bank may have. Indeed, global loans are to be applied to the financing of a specific agreed-upon investment plan in accordance with acceptable standards of project selection. Therefore, development banks which borrow from BID must submit periodic reports so that BID will know whether or not the program for which it lent is being carried out. The periodic reports, submitted either quarterly, semi-annually, or annually according to prior agreement, are divided into three groups:

a. Financial position of the institution at the close of the business year. This includes basic financial statements, balance sheets, operating statements, with necessary annexes to make possible a proper analysis of the development bank's position;

b. financial projections showing the forecast of operations in subsequent years; and

c. an investment plan which serves to outline the proposed use of the BID loan.

Like IFC, BID also has a maximum amount of sub-loans which can be made by the bank without prior approval of BID. If the sub-loan exceeds this limit, it must be submitted to BID but only after it has been approved by the board of directors of the borrowing bank. BID always reserves the right to request supplementary information and to raise objections to certain operations for such reasons as the following:

a. Duplication of another direct operation which BID is studying or has approved.

b. Disagreement as to the priority of the sub-loan in question.

c. The need to consider additional technical, economic, or financial factors on the basis of more complete information.

Procurement policies on BID loans to development banks permit procurement of goods and services on a world-wide

Table 8

Export-Import Bank
Financial Assistance to Intermediate Credit Institutions
(January, 1960 - December, 1964)

Development Bank	Amount (in millions)	Date	Int. Rate	Term (Yrs.)	Grace (Yrs.)
Argentina					
1. Banco Industrial de la República	5	12-60	5-3/4	8	3
2. Banco Industrial de la República	5	12-60	5-3/4	8	3
Colombia					
3. Corporación Colombiana de Desarrollo	.5	3-60	5-3/4	5	1-1/2
Chile					
4. Banco Central de Chile	5	9-60	5-3/4	8	2
5. Banco Central de Chile	15	3-64	5-1/2	8	2
Dominican Republic					
6. Corporación de Fomento de la República Dominicana	1	12-62	5-3/4	7	2
Italy					
7. Istituto Mobiliare Italiano	20	12-64	4-3/4	7	2

Table 8, Continued

Export-Import Bank
Financial Assistance to Intermediate Credit Institutions
(January, 1960 - December, 1964)

Development Bank	Amount (in millions)	Date	Int. Rate	Term (Yrs.)	Grace (Yrs.)
Japan					
8. Industrial Bank of Japan	25	1-61	5-1/2	7	2
Jamaica					
9. Development Finance Corp.	5	3-63	5-3/4	6-1/2	2
Mexico					
10. Cía. Central de Aceptaciones	2	4-63	5-3/4	7	2
Pakistan					
11. Industrial Development Bank	2.5	2-63	5-3/4	6-1/2	2
Peru					
12. Banco Industrial del Peru	2.5	6-60	5-3/4	9	2
Spain					
13. Banco Industrial de Bilbao	10	7-64	4-3/4	7	1
14. Banco de Crédito Industrial	2.5	4-61	5-1/2	6	1

Table 8, Continued

Export-Import Bank
Financial Assistance to Intermediate Credit Institutions
(January, 1960 - December, 1964)

Development Bank	Amount (in millions)	Date	Int. Rate	Term (Yrs.)	Grace (Yrs.)
Uruguay					
15. Banco de la República Oriental del Uruguay	5	11-62	5-3/4	6.5	2
Venezuela					
16. Corp. Venezolana de Fomento	7.5	8-61	5-3/4	6.5	2
TOTAL:	113.5				

Source: Annual Reports - Export-Import Bank

basis, exclusive of the Sino-Soviet block, except in cases where it is clearly inappropriate, such as for the expansion of a project requiring equipment from the manufacturer of the existing installation.

BID will continue in the future to be a major supplier of credits for development banks in Latin America. As the ability of the various countries in Latin America to articulate well-defined projects increases, it is probable that BID lending to development banks will become a declining proportion of the then current levels of BID resources. However, these resources are expected to increase and the estimated volume of BID lending to development banks will therefore probably increase in absolute terms.

Export-Import Bank

The principal purpose of the Export-Import Bank, which was chartered in 1934 in an abortive effort to finance trade with Russia, is to assist in the financing of the U.S. export trade. The Export-Import Bank, during the period of January, 1960, to December, 1964, lent $113.5 million to intermediate credit institutions for relending to sub-borrowers for purchases of goods manufactured in the United States.

For the Export-Import Bank to lend to a development bank is a rather roundabout way of achieving its purposes, yet because many development banks over a period of one to two years have been able to place the funds lent by the Export-Import Bank, in purchases in the United States, the Export-Import Bank has continued and expanded this practice.

As one can see from Table 8, the average loan by the Export-Import Bank to an intermediate credit institution is about $5 million and the interest rate for the past few years has been 5.5 per cent. Generally, the terms run between six and nine years with a grace period between one and three years.

The geographical pattern of lending finds that almost half the credits have been extended to Latin America with the balance divided almost equally between Europe and the Far East (see Table 8). Both the Near East and Africa have not received much Export-Import Bank assistance through development banks.

The bank operates on the following principles (and any development bank which can satisfy the Export-Import Bank can expect an opportunity to obtain a line of credit on the above terms):

a.   The bank's primary purpose is to promote the U.S. export and import trade. The bank, therefore, does not place primary emphasis on the contribution its financing will make to economic or social development, but rather on the contribution it will make to the promotion of the trade of the United States. At the present time the bank's programs relate almost exclusively to assisting export trade rather than import trade because of the ready availability of financing for imports.

b.   The bank does not compete with private capital. Therefore the bank will not provide assistance for those export transactions where financing from private sources on reasonable terms is available.

c.   The loans of the bank shall generally be made for specific purposes, although in some cases lines of credit have been extended to development banks where the precise details of the projects to be financed were not available at the time of the signing of the loan. In each case, however, there was a general agreement as to how the loan would be used.

d.   The bank must have reasonable assurance of repayment. This criterion relates both to the ability of the borrower to secure income to service the debt as well as to the ability of the borrower to obtain foreign exchange sufficient to repay the debt. The bank expects its loan to be repaid on time and in dollars. Therefore it examines the credit standing of the particular borrower involved and also the ability of the country in which the borrower is located to provide the necessary dollars with which the borrower can repay the loan.

Indeed, all of the countries with which the Export-Import Bank deals are rated from A to D according to the evaluation of the bank's staff of the ability of the country to service a debt in dollars.

The financing provided by the bank through these loans is available for the payment of technical services in addition to payment for the cost of machinery and equipment. The source of the technical services and of the machinery and equipment is restricted to the United States of America.

The borrower, under a loan from the Export-Import Bank, will, as in the case of a loan from AID, be required to ship all products financed by the bank on United States Flag carriers unless a waiver is obtained from the appropriate authorities to the effect that United States vessels are not available in sufficient numbers or in sufficient tonnage capacity or in sufficient time or at reasonable rates.

While the bank is interested in obtaining maximum security on its loans it usually does not take a mortgage. However, it may take other forms of security such as equipment liens, foreign bank guarantee, collateral in the form of stocks, bonds, or other aspects or some other arrangements. The loan agreement may also prohibit the borrower from mortgaging the property unless he secures the bank. Bank loans are repayable in dollars and the bank will generally, in the case of a loan to a private borrower, require that the appropriate governmental authorities have approved the project and have given their assurances that the dollar exchange necessary to repay the principal and interest on the loan will be made available as the loan payments become due.

The bank has no formal loan procedures but has prepared a list of information which it will require in the consideration of a loan application, which we have included as Appendix B.

The list of information required was designed to fit the normal kind of project which the Export-Import Bank finances, that is, one which is clearly capable of breakdown into its various elements. A loan to a development bank must be justified to the Export-Import Bank in as much detail as pos-sible according to the list, but clearly some modifications must be obtained since it is hardly likely that a development bank will find it feasible to submit all of the details on each project even if these details were available to and known by the bank at the time it was soliciting a loan from the Export-Import Bank.

It appears that the present volume and rate of Export-Import Bank lending through development banks will remain about the same for the near future. There does not appear to be any significant reason why the present level should change.

Agency for International Development

To describe briefly such a complex organization as the Agency for International Development is a difficult task, even when we are relating it to the assistance that it may have in the past rendered and in the future be capable of rendering just to development banking. Nevertheless we have attempted to set out in Appendix B the pattern of assistance in considerable detail which AID has rendered to development banks.

As one can see, the impact has been extensive both in magnitude and in scope. The AID assistance to private industrial and agricultural projects through intermediate credit institutions totals approximately $1,164 million. Of this total, industry has received by far the lion's share: about $958 million, with agriculture coming in for $201 million. By region, the Near East and South Asia (NESA) has received the most financial assistance, $518 million, which has predominantly been made up of assistance to industry of $448 million. Assistance to agriculture has been $70 million in the NESA region. Latin America and the Far East are almost even from the standpoint of AID financial assistance through development banks, but in Latin America the assistance has been divided $197 million to industry and $108 million to agriculture, whereas in the Far East the assistance has been divided $285 million to industry and $11 million to agriculture. Assistance to Africa through development banks has been comparatively small: only $39 million in all, $26 million being extended through banks specified for industrial relending and $12 million specified for agricultural relending.

There are five general categories of assistance through which AID has been able to relate to the financial growth of development banks as follows:

a.   Development Loans

One of the most significant ways, especially for the future, that AID can relate to development banking is through the extension of development loans for relending to qualified private borrowers. In the Near East South Asia region, the interest rates for these loans for industrial relending are about 4.5 to 5.5 per cent with terms ranging from 10 to 15 years. Grace periods on

these loans in the NESA region have ranged from zero to
five years. In the Latin American and African regions
the terms have been somewhat softer for industrial relending. In Latin America, interest rates have ranged
from 2 to 4.5 per cent with one loan at 5.75 per cent
and terms have been longer, 15 to 20 years, with grace
periods consistently at 5 years with one exception of
10 years. In Africa dollar loans for industrial relending
have been usually made at 3 to 4 per cent for 15 years
but between one- and five-year grace periods. The only
region in which AID has had a significant impact on development banks which lend to private agricultural projects is Latin America, in which, as mentioned above,
$108 million has been extended to 11 institutions. Here
the terms are somewhat softer, with 6 of the 11 institutions assisted receiving terms up to 40 years with 10
years' grace.

Dollar loans are with some exceptions restricted to
procurement within the United States and the loan agreement or subsequent letters of implementation usually
spell out the categories of sub-loans which are permitted
without prior AID approval. AID usually tries to dis-
suade the sub-borrower from the development bank from
lending for projects which:

(i) Produce goods for export which are currently
in world surplus

(ii) Produce goods for export in competition with
United States goods in U.S. domestic markets

(iii) In some agreements there is prohibition against
the use of the loan funds for sub-loans which result in luxury production. However, this prohibition is not contained in other loan agreements
and, indeed, development banks have used AID
funds for sub-loans to soft drink manufacturers,
to beer manufacturers, and to manufacturers of
hosiery and cosmetics

Along with other major international public sources
of capital, AID requires that the borrower submit
periodic reports adequate to indicate the financial status
of the development bank and adequate to indicate the use

Key: Private ownership   - P
     Government ownership - G
     Mixed ownership   - M

Table 9

Agency for International Development Financial Assistance to Development Banks
To June 30, 1964
(In millions of dollars)

Country	Bank	Owner-ship	Total Finan. Assist-ance	Dollar Loans	Yrs.	% Int. Rate	Term Grace	Dollar Grants	Date	Local Cur-rency Loans	Date	% Int. Rate	Term Grace	Local Cur-rency Grants	Date
NEAR EAST	INDUSTRIAL RELENDING (TOTALS)		$448.5	$123.5	.....	.....	.....	$7.1	.....	$271.2	.....	.....	.....	$46.7	.....
Greece	Economic Development Financing Organization....	(G)	98	5	62	4-1/2	15-5	.....	.....	93	58	4	40-4	.....	.....
	National Bank of Greece ...	(P)	5	5	62	4-1/2	15-5	.....	.....					.....	.....
India	ICICI	(P)	26	5	61	5	15-0	.....	.....	21	59-62	5	40-4	.....	.....
	IFC....	(M-G)	51	30	60-62	5	15-1	.....	.....	21	59-62	5	40-4	.....	.....
	National Small Industries Corp....	(G)	10	10	60	5	10-0	.....	.....					.....	.....
	Refinance Corp. for Industry....	(G)	55	.....				.....	.....	55	59-62	4	40-4	.....	.....
Iran	IMDBI....	(P)	5.2	5.2	59	5-3/4	15-0	.....	.....				20-0	.....	.....
Israel	IDB	(M-P)	72	20	59-61	5	10-0	.....	.....	52	59-64	4-5	30-4	.....	.....
Jordan	Industrial Development Fund	(G)	1.1	.....				1.1	55	.....				.....	.....
	Jordan Central Coopera-tive Union....	(P)	5.5	.....				.....	.....					.5	62
	Municipal Loan Fund....	(G)	3	.....				2.8	57	.....				.2	63
Lebanon	BCAIF....	(M-P)	5	5	59	.....	.....	.....	.....	.....				.....	.....
Nepal	NIDC....	(M-G)	5	1.4	61-63	4-1/2 to 5	15-3	1.3	56	2.0	61-64	4-1/2 to 5	15-3	.2	64

Country	Bank	Ownership	Total Finan. Assistance	Dollar Loans	Yrs.	% Int. Rate	Term Grace	Dollar Grants	Date	Local Currency Loans	Date	% Int. Rate	Term Grace	Local Currency Grants	Date
Pakistan	PICIC............(P)		$ 34	$21.7	58-62	5	7-0	......	......	$ 6.3	59-63	4	30-4	$ 6.3	58-63
	IDB..............(G)		6.3	......				......	......	6.3	59-63	4	30-4	......	......
	Small Industries Corp. ....(G)		2.1	......				......	......	2.1	59	4	30-4	......	......
Syria	Industrial Bank ....(G)		.2	.2	60	5	10-0	......	......	......				......	......
Turkey	IDB..............(P)		55.5	15	58-62	5-1/2	15-0	$1.9	57	12.5	63-64	4-6	......	38	62-61
	4 Other Turkish Banks.....(G)		13.0	......			10-0			......				1.5	61
NEAR EAST AGRICULTURE RELENDING (TOTALS)			$ 69.9	$66.6				$2.1						$67.8	......
Afghanistan	Agriculture and Cottage Industries Bank.........(G)		.035	......				......	......	......				.035	60
Greece	Agriculture Bank of Greece (G)		60.9	......				......	......	......				60.9	62
Jordan	Agriculture Loan Fund.... (G)		2.1	......				2.1	58	......				......	......
Turkey	Agriculture Bank..........(G)		6.9	......				......	......	......				6.9	57-62
LATIN AMERICA INDUSTRIAL RELENDING (TOTALS)			$197.6	$66.6				$2		$129.0					......
Bolivia	Banco Industrial............(P)		2.7	2.4	58-63	2-1/4	20-5	......		.3	63	N.A.	N.A.	......	......
	Banco Minero de Bolivia...(G)		.4	......				......		.4	62	N.A.	N.A.	......	......
Brazil	BNDE.................(G)		94.8	4	53-63	3-1/4	20-5	......		94.8	57-63	4	35-4	......	......
	COPEG Development Bank (M-G)		4	4	53-63	3-1/4	20-5	......		......				......	......

Table 9, Continued

Country	Bank	Owner-ship	Total Finan. Assist-ance	Dollar Loans	Yrs.	% Int. Rate	Term Grace	Dollar Grants	Date	Local Cur-rency Loans	Date	% Int. Rate	Term Grace	Local Cur-rency Grants	Date
Colombia	Banco de la Republica (Private Investment)	(G)	$40	$10	64	5-1/2	15-5	......	......	$30	63	......	......	......	......
Costa Rica	COFISA	(P)	5	5	64	4-1/4	20-5	......	......	......	......	......	......	......	......
Ecuador	National Development Bank	(G)	2.9	......	......	......	......	......	......	2.9	56-57	4	12-4	......	......
	National Securities Commission	(G)	5	5	62	5-3/4	20-5	......	......	......	......	......	......	......	......
El Salvador	INSAFI	(G)	4.5	4.5	63	......	25-10	......	......	......	......	......	......	......	......
	Financiera de Desarrollo e Inversiones	(P)	5.2	5.2	64	2	20-5	......	......	......	......	......	......	......	......
Honduras	Financiera Hondurena	(P)	5	5	64	2	20-5	......	......	......	......	......	......	......	......
Panama	Desarrollo Industrial	(P)	5	5	64	......	20-5	......	......	......	......	......	......	......	......
Paraguay	Banco Central del Para-guay	(G)	.6	......	......	......	......	......	......	.6	63	4	22-4	......	......
Uruguay	Banco de la Republica Oriental	(G)	3	3	64	3-1/2	25-5	......	......	......	......	......	......	......	......
Regional	CABEI	(G)	19.5	17.5	62-64	3/4	40-10	$2	61-62	......	......	......	......	......	......
LATIN AMERICA AGRICULTURAL RELENDING (TOTALS)			$108.3	$98.2	......	......	......	......	......	$2.5	......	......	......	$7.6	......
Bolivia	Agricultural Bank	(G)	11.3	3.7	63	3/4	40-10	......	......	......	......	......	......	......	......

Country	Bank	Ownership	Total Finan. Assistance	Dollar Loans	Yrs.	% Int. Rate	Term Grace	Dollar Grants	Date	Local Currency Loans	Date	% Int. Rate	Term Grace	Local Currency Grants	Date
Colombia	Casa de Credito Agrario	(G)	$ 8	$8	61	4	20-10								
	INCORA	(G)	10	10	63	3/4	40-10								
	Banco Ganadero	(M-P)	4	4	64	2-1/2	20-5								
Costa Rica	Banco Nacional de Costa Rica	(G)	10	10	61-63	3-1/2	20-0								
Dominican Republic	Banco Agricola	(G)	2.5							$2.5	62	3/4	20-0		
El Salvador	Banco Central de la Reserva	(G)	8.9	8.9	63	3/4	30-10								
Guatemala	Banco de Guatemala	(G)	5	5	59	3	14-1								
Mexico	Nacional Financiera	(G)	20	20	62	3/4	40-10								
Paraguay	Banco de Fomento	(G)	3	3	64	3/4	40-10								
Peru	Institute of Agrarian Reform and Colonization	(G)	15.6	15.6	61-64	3/4	40-10								
Venezuela	Agricultural and Livestock Bank	(G)	10	10	62	3/4	20-5								
LATIN AMERICA - COOPERATIVE RELENDING (TOTALS)			$ 4.95	$4.95										$ .15	
Ecuador	Banco de Cooperativas del Ecuador	(P)	1.3	1.2	64	3/4	25-10							.15	64

Table 9, Continued

Country	Bank	Owner-ship	Total Finan. Assist-ance	Dollar Loans	Yrs.	% Int. Rate	Term Grace	Dollar Grants	Date	Local Cur-rency Loans	Date	% Int. Rate	Term Grace	Local Cur-rency Grants	Date
Chile	Instituto de Financia-miento Cooperativo	(P)	$ 3.65	$ 3.65	65	N.A.	N.A.								
AFRICA	INDUSTRIAL RELEND-ING (TOTALS)		$26.5	$18.5						$ 7.1				$ .9	
Dahomey	DBD	(G)	.7							.7	62	3/4	40-10		
Ethiopia	DBE	(G)	2	2	61	4	15-1								
Ivory Coast	BIDI	(P)	5	5	64	4	20-5								
Kenya	IDC	(G)	.14											.14	59-64
	Ministry of Commerce	(G)	.29											.29	
Niger	Development Bank	(G)	.5	.5	63	4	15-3								
Nigeria	Revolving Loan Fund	(G)	.5											.5	59
Somali	Credito Somalo	(G)	2	2	59	4	15-0								
Sudan	IDB	(G)	2	2	62	3-1/4	15-3								
Tunisia	STB	(G)	11.4	5	61	4	15-1			6.4	58-62	4	30-4		
Uganda	UDC	(M-G)	2	2	63	3-1/4	15-3								
AFRICA	AGRICULTURAL RELENDING (TOTALS)		$12.6	$ 5.0						$ 6.5				$ 1.1	

136

Country	Bank	Ownership	Total Finan. Assistance	Dollar Loans	Yrs.	% Int. Rate	Term Grace	Dollar Grants	Date	Local Currency Loans	Date	% Int. Rate	Term Grace	Local Currency Grants	Date
Kenya	Board of Agriculture	(G)	$ .35	.....	.....	.....	.....	.....		.....		.....	.....	$ .35	.....
Libya	National Agriculture Bank	(G)	.7	.....	.....	.....	.....	.....		.....		.....	.....	.7	59-63
Tunisia	Banque Nationale Agricole	(G)	11.5	$ 5	61	4	.....	.....		$ 6.5	60-62	4	27-4	.....	.....
FAR EAST	INDUSTRIAL RELENDING (TOTALS)		$285.9	$23.1				$46.6		$169.4				$ 46.8	.....
Cambodia	Caisse Nationale d'Equipement	(G)	2	.....	.....	.....	.....	.....		.....		.....	.....	2	60
	Royal Office of Corporations	(G)	1.3	.....	.....	.....	.....	.....		.....		.....	.....	1.3	53
China	Bank of Communications	(G)	.9	.....	.....	.....	.....	.....		.9	63-64	9	8-0	.....	.....
	CDC	(P)	20	10	60	5	10-0	.....		10.0	60-62	6	30-0	.....	.....
	Land Bank Corporation	(G)	.68	.68	58	3/4	5-0	.....		.....		.....	.....	.....	.....
	Overseas Chinese Commercial Bank Small Industry Loan Fund	(P)	.25	.....	.....	.....	.....	.....		.25	60-62	6	3-0	.....	.....
	Fund	(G)	13	2.4	59	5	5-0	6.7	54	3.9	60-63	9	8-0	.....	.....
Korea	Medium Industry Bank	(G)	14.2	.....	.....	.....	.....	8.2	57	6.0	57-59	2	30-5	.....	.....
	Reconstruction Bank	(G)	181	5	59	5	10-0	21.0	57-59	134.4	62-63	8	35-5	20.6	62
	Small Industry Development	(G)	3.8	.....	.....	.....	.....	3.8	57	.....		.....	.....	.....	.....

Table 9, Continued

Country	Bank	Owner-ship	Total Finan. Assist-ance	Dollar Loans						Local Currency Loans				Local Currency Grants	Date
				Loans	Yrs.	% Int. Rate	Term Grace	Dollar Grants	Date	Loans	Date	% Int. Rate	Term Grace		
Philippines	Central Bank (Industrial Guarantees)...	(G)	$21.6	......				......						$21.6	......
	Central Bank (Small Industry)...	(G)	5	$ 5	59	5	7-1	......							
	Development Bank of Philippines...	(G)	6.2	......				......		$ 6.2	58	4	17-4	......	
	PDC ...	(P)	7.0	......				......		7.0	63	1/2	30-15	......	
Thailand	IFC ...	(P)	.75	......				......		.75	62	N.A.	N.A.	......	
Vietnam	Industrial Development Center ...	(G)	8.2	......				$6.9	58	......				1.3	58
FAR EAST	AGRICULTURAL RE-LENDING (TOTALS)		$11.0	......						$ 6.8	......			$ 4.2	......
Indonesia	Bank for Cooperatives	(P)	.04	......						......				.04	64
Korea	National Agricultural Cooperative Federation...	(P)	6.8	......						6.8	62	3	30-5	......	
Philippines	Rural Bank Trust...	(G)	4.2	......						......				4.2	53

Source: Unpublished unofficial AID statistics released September, 1964, by AID/DFPE

being made of the loan proceeds. Projects involving AID funds over a certain amount are required to be submitted to AID in Washington for approval. It is both in the reporting process and the sub-loan approval process that AID and the other international lenders appear to be killing two birds with one stone. First, they are ensuring that they are kept informed and that their loan is in this manner and to this extent protected; secondly, they are educating the management of the borrower with respect to project analysis.

Although in the beginning most borrowers find AID reporting and sub-loan approval requirements rather onerous, they realize eventually that these requirements benefit them as well as protect AID. The requirement of AID review of projects over a certain amount gives the development bank additional leverage to resist political pressure for a sub-loan in that a development bank would confidently expect AID to refuse to approve clearly uneconomic projects.

There are other minor restrictions on the use of AID dollar loans, such as the requirement that half of the goods purchased by proceeds of the loan be shipped in United States Flag vessels. Also, there is the requirement that marine insurance be purchased in the United States and that purchases be made only after competitive bids are solicited and small business in the United States circularized.

b.   Dollar Grants

Dollar grants to development banks will be used in the future to a decreasing extent, if at all. The only dollar grant which has been made available to development banks since 1959 has been a grant of $2 million over the period of 1961-62 to the Central American Bank for Economic Integration (CABEI). The purpose of the grant was to cover some of the expenses of the bank during its initial period of operations.

Dollar grants are subject to much the same restrictions as to use, procurement, and the like as dollar loans so there is no need to repeat what we have mentioned above. A development bank would be wise to explore the possibility, if dollar resources are required, that AID should extend it a dollar grant. However, the likelihood as one can see from Table 9, is not great.

c.   Local Currency Loans

These are loans which are made in some cases by
AID alone, and in other cases jointly by the host government and by AID.   The funds usually arise from the sale
of U.S. surplus agricultural products in the host country
or from local currency counterparts of AID Program
Loans to the host country government.

The use of local currency generated from the sale of
U.S. surplus products in that country under U.S. Public
Law 480 or generated under any other program is the
subject of prior agreement between the governments of
the respective countries as to broad categories of spend-
ing.   U.S. Public Law 480 under which these currencies
are generated has many titles to which a certain amount
of proceeds of a Public Law 480 sale are allocated in
advance.   Individuals organizing a development bank or
officials of a development bank interested in obtaining
local currency for expenditures for use by the bank would
be wise to consult with officials of AID and of the host
government at a very early stage to determine whether
there is any local currency available under Public Law
480 and precisely how the funds are approved for release.
In most cases both AID and the host country must agree
to the uses to which the funds will be put.

d.   Local Currency Grants

As one can see from Table 9, local currency grants
have also been rather sparingly used.   The tendency is to
move away from the grant form of assistance in all its
forms to the loan form of assistance.   Yet grants still
are available.   For example, local currency grants were
made in 1962 to the agricultural bank in Turkey and the
agricultural bank in Bolivia, in 1963 to the Banco Nacional de la Vivienda in the Dominican Republic, the Municipal
Loan Fund in Jordan, the Industrial Development Corporation in Kenya, the Kenya Board of Agriculture, and the
Bank for Cooperatives in Indonesia and Ecuador.

Local Currency grants can be justified by development banks on the grounds that such grants will help them
over the first few years of operation.   During this period
loan values and interest revenues are small, a fact which

usually produces a deficit in operating revenues. Such a grant will help a bank obtain the kind of assistance it needs in order to accomplish its purposes and objectives.

e.   The Investment Guarantee Program

The investment guarantee program, as one can see from Table 10, has been of assistance to development banks in that it has facilitated lending by U. S. private commercial banks and Edge Act companies to development banks.

The guarantee program is open to corporations, partnerships, citizens, or any other associations created under the laws of the United States or any state or territory in the United States and substantially beneficially owned by citizens of the United States. The investor may also be a wholly owned foreign subsidiary of an eligible United States corporation.

Three separate kinds of guarantee programs are available:

(i)   Specific political-risk guarantees against

    a) inconvertibility of foreign currency
    b) expropriation or confiscation
    c) loss due to war, revolution, or insurrection

(ii)   Extended-risk guarantees which cover up to 75 per cent of both political and business risks

(iii) Extended-risk guarantees covering up to 100 per cent of losses on pilot or demonstration private housing projects

This latter guarantee program need not concern us since development bank activity usually does not include relending for the financing of houses, although, indeed, a development bank may relend for housing construction.

Before a guarantee can be issued for an investment in a particular country, its government must sign an agreement with the United States to institute the guarantee program. AID provides on request a current list of the countries with whom it has already signed guarantee agreements. There is a provision in the current foreign assistance act that aid will be terminated to countries which have not signed a guarantee agreement with the United States covering the political risks mentioned above by a certain cut-off date.

The guarantee when issued is in the form of a contract between the investor and AID and is backed by the full faith and credit of the United States Government. The standard formal contract is available upon request from AID.

In general, projects must be approved by AID as furthering the economic development and productive capacities of less developed countries. This includes most projects which promote trade, increase production, raise standards of living, and improve technical efficiency. At the present time there is no restriction as to the size of investments which may be guaranteed and contracts have been written for as little as $1,000 or for as much as $63 million and for a maximum term of 20 years.

Before any investment guarantee contract is issued, AID requires the investor to secure approval from the foreign government for the inclusion of his project under the investment guarantee agreement. It is the responsibility of the investor to present to the foreign government the plan and details of the investment and to fulfill the foreign government's requirements regarding the investment and to request the foreign government's written expression to the U.S. AID Mission or the U.S. Embassy of the approval of the project for investment guarantee purposes. When the investor has obtained such approval and when the terms of a proposal are clearly understood by AID to meet the criteria, the application for a guarantee then receives intensive review in AID. If approved, the guarantee contract is then executed on behalf of the United States Government by AID.

AID is interested in guaranteeing loans made by banks, insurance companies, and Edge Act companies to development banks where it is clearly demonstrable that such loans will lead to the establishment, expansion, or modernization of productive facilities. Loans which in effect refinance or pay off outstanding indebtedness or which provide funds for distribution to owners, partners, or share holders normally will not be eligible for a guarantee of any kind, either political risk or extended risk, nor will guarantees be available to cover loans, the primary purpose of which is to effect a change in ownership in the enterprise or to provide funds for speculation in any kind of property, real or personal.

Except in unusual circumstances guarantees will be made only in connection with projects which involve procurement of United States goods and services, in amounts substantially equal to the amount of the guarantee. Loans will not be guaranteed if the necessary private financing is available or if an acceptable alternative guarantee is otherwise available or if the project may result in unacceptable effect on the U.S. economy or the United States balance of payments.

In the case of the extended risk guarantee where 75 per cent only of an investor's commitment is protected, AID will consider proposals for applying this guarantee against the later maturities of a loan while allowing the percentage of the loan not covered by such a guarantee to constitute the early maturities. For example, if one assumes that AID was prepared to guarantee 75 per cent of the loan, they would in effect be guaranteeing none of the risks for installments equal to the first 25 per cent of the principal due, and 100 per cent of the remainder of the installments.

For the extended risk coverage, the fee charged is payable annually in advance not to exceed 1.75 per cent of the amount of the extended risk guarantee to be in force on the estimated amount of the disbursed and outstanding credit. The fee for the political risk is 0.5 per cent of the amount of each of the three coverages in force in any given contract year. There is also an annual fee of 0.25 per cent the amount of each standby coverage, that is, the difference between the amount in force and the maximum amount which the investor may elect to have put in force on each of the three coverages.

Table 10

Status of AID Guarantees Covering U. S. Private Investment
in Intermediate Credit Institutions
(as of June 30, 1964)

Bank	Investor	Amount of Coverage	Type of Guarantee
COLOMBIA			
1. Financiera del Valle	Continental International Finance Corp.	1.010 mill	
PERU			
2. PERUINVEST	Morgan Guarantee International Banking Corp.	.632 mill	
CHINA			
3. China Development Corp.	Morgan Guarantee International Banking Corp.	.800 mill	usually divided equally between convertibility and expropriation
IVORY COAST			
4. Societe Ivoirienne de Banque	Morgan Guarantee International Banking Corp.	.656 mill	

Bank	Investor	Amount of Coverage	Type of Guarantee
MOROCCO			
5. Banque Nationale pour le Developpement Economique	Morgan Guarantee International Banking Corp.	.400 mill	usually
TUNISIA			
6. Banque d'Escompte et de Credit et Industrie en Tunisie	Morgan Guarantee International Banking Corp.	.578 mill	divided
7. Union International de Banques	Bank of America	.153	between
TURKEY			
8. Americo Turk-Is Tico set Bankasi	Bank of America	.501	controvertibility and expropriation

f.   AID Policy with Regard to Development Banks

Information required by AID in order to consider a loan to a development bank is found in Appendix C. As a general rule AID will encourage the establishment and growth of sound development banks where there is a demonstrative need for such institutions. In the case of a dollar loan, both AID and the host country have to agree that such a loan is both of sufficient high priority within a country program and, also, meets AID's normal lending criteria, such as reasonable prospects of repayment, nonavailability of other free world capital, etc.

AID has in the past worked closely with U.S. and other free world private and international banking interests in the establishment and operation of development banks, such as the Industrial Development Bank of Turkey, the Industrial Mining and Development Bank of Iran, PICIC, and ICICI.

AID feels that the key to success for a development bank lies in its management. Consequently, it must have reasonable assurance that the personnel who will be responsible for the management of the bank are competent. AID looks very closely at the board of directors and expects it to be composed of men of stature representing a broad segment of the business community. AID feels that it is important in the beginning years of a bank for foreign advisors to work with bank personnel, training them in the tasks that they are able to perform.

As mentioned above, the ownership of a bank (private, government, or mixed) is not a problem to AID lending as it is in the case of the World Bank family. On the other hand, AID officials point out that in the case of sole government or joint private/government ownership, AID will encourage the government to divest itself of its holdings in the bank at the earliest practicable time. In any event, AID officials feel that it is in the interest of the bank that it obtain a reasonable degree of autonomy to ensure insulation from undue political pressure.

AID avoids ownership of foreign assets and, consequently, has not invested in equity shares of development banks although, legally, it probably could receive

convertible debentures. If such debentures are converted into stock, however, AID will sell this stock in order
to avoid owning equity. The author knows of no instance
where AID has obtained such convertible debenture
positions.

AID in general expects that the loan made will be an
amount sufficient to cover the expected lending activity
of the development bank over an 18 to 24-month period
with the understanding that: (1) when the loan has been
committed, (2) the bank's effectiveness proven, and
(3) the need for additional finances demonstrated, AID
might be sympathetic to the consideration of a second
"tranche." After two or possibly three injections of seed
capital on concessional terms, AID would expect the institution to be able to bear the market rates.

The terms and conditions of AID loans necessarily
vary depending upon a number of factors. The interest
rate is usually set so that the rate charged by the bank
can bear a reasonable relationship to the local interest
rate structure of the type of sub-loan contemplated.
Bearing in mind the bank's need to generate earnings
sufficient to meet administrative costs to attract increased investment and to make a contribution to economic development, AID realizes that for new development banks a special problem exists in meeting expenses
in the early years. It often works with the organizing
committee of a bank to obtain other local governmental
assistance in the form of subsidies, such as long-term
loans at little or no interest, assistance with administrative costs, tax benefits, etc.

In addition to the many kinds of financial assistance
above, AID can also provide technical assistance to assist development banks. In the first place, AID can arrange to send a survey team to the host country to study
with the organizing group of the bank the need for such a
bank and details as to its organization and implementation. Such a team normally makes recommendations regarding the relative urgency of supporting such a bank,
what kind of a bank should be formed, and how it should
operate. Second, AID can assist managements of development banks by providing U.S. or third-country experts to the institution for training or in certain cases

bring selected host country personnel to the U.S. or to third countries for training.

With respect to the cost of technical assistance, AID is increasingly holding to a policy requiring that technical assistance be paid for out of the loan. In smaller loans this is often a formidable burden. AID in such cases will explore the possibility that the loan might be made from AID to the host government and the host government will lend an amount smaller by the amount of the technical assistance to the bank, thus assuming itself the financial responsibility for the technical assistance to the bank. In larger loans, of course, costs of technical assistance are much smaller in proportion to the total amount of the loan and may be borne by the institution itself. Third, AID can also assist in the establishment and improvement of permanent development centers either within or separate from the bank. AID's present policy is to separate these development centers from the development bank because of the danger that the same personnel who work with an investor to develop a project will, indeed, be approving the project for a loan. AID does not feel that such a procedure is a sufficient guarantee of objectivity in loan analysis.

Other Public Assistance

A development bank seeking finances for initiation or growth should not overlook other public sources of finance from governments and other institutions outside the United States. The assistance programs of many governments may be a more responsive source of capital than AID or any other public or international source. The assistance programs of the United Kingdom, France, Germany, Netherlands, Belgium, Italy, and Japan, to name a few, have assisted development banks throughout the world.

Both United Kingdom and France have had geographic limitations to their assistance, the United Kingdom assisting the Commonwealth and depending territories through the Commonwealth Development Corporation (CDC) and France to the French Community through Caisse Centrale de Cooperation Economique (CCCE).

Germany, through the Kreditanstalt for Wiederaufbau,

has made credits available to IFC in India, ICICI in India and
Nepal Industrial Development Corporation, development
banks in Cameroons and Pakistan, Kenya, and Tanganyika
The Netherlands has made a loan to a development bank in
Surinam, and Belgium has extended credits to a bank in Congo.
Italy, through Istituto Mobiliare Italiano, has made available
credits to a Liberian bank. Japan has invested chiefly through
a consortium of private development banks in India, Thailand,
Malaysia, and Nigeria.

Terms and conditions under which assistance can be extended will naturally vary from institution to institution but
should bear some similarity and should require information
similar to that required by AID, or the World Bank, or BID.
A development bank interested in relating to one of these institutions should explore with them directly the terms and
conditions on which they would participate.

Foreign Private Financial Assistance to Development Banks

There are many private financial institutions which have
in the past rendered financial assistance to development banks
or which offer a potential for financial assistance to development banks in the future.

One can see from Tables 11 and 12 that quite a number of financial institutions all over the world have provided
both debt and equity to development banks. These institutions
frequently participate in loans made to development banks by
public and international lending agencies, such as the World
Bank, the Inter-American Development Bank, the Export-
Import Bank, and the like. These public and international
lending agencies like to obtain participations so that their own
money will go further. In view of the relatively small
amounts involved in participations one must conclude that
this motive is weak. Obtaining of these participations is also
looked upon as a way of leading the private financial community gradually into the business of international investment and
is a method demonstrating the soundness of a particular investment.

The Inter-American Development Bank, for example, offers for participation many of the loans that it makes from its
Ordinary Fund. It must send out 170 letters to various

Table 11

Selected Private Commercial Bank and U.S. Edge Act
Corporation Investment in Selected Development Banks

1. Bank of America (U.S.)

Equity	Debt
	Early maturities, 5-3/4 - 5-1/2% IADB or IBRD loans:
PICIC (Pakistan)	Banco Agrícola y Pecuario
ICICI (India)	(Venezuela)
IFC (Thailand)	Banco de la Nación (Argentina)
PDC (Philippines)	tina)
MDFL (Malaysia)	Nacional Financiera (2)
NIDB (Nigeria)	(Mexico)
Investment Bank (Athens)	CORFO (Chile)
	Corporación Venezolana de Fomento (Venezuela)
	ICICI (India)

2. Irving International Financing Corporation (U.S.)

Equity	Debt
	Early maturities, 5-3/4 - 5-1/2% IADB or IBRD loans (as Irving Trust Co.)
PDC (Philippines)	Banco de Costa Rica
Industrialization Fund	(Costa Rica)
Co. (Finland)	Nacional Financiera (2)
NIDB (Nigeria)	(Mexico)
	CORFO (Chile)
	Banco de Guatemala (Guatemala)
	Instituto de Fomento Nacional (Nicaragua)
	Corporación Venezolana de Fomento (2)(Venezuela)

Table 11, Continued

Irving International Financing Corporation(U.S.)--cont'd

Equity	Debt
	Banco Nacional de Nicaragua (Nicaragua)
	Austrian Investment Credit Corporation (Austria)

3. Manufacturers Hanover International Financing Corporation (U.S.)

Equity	Debt
	Early maturities, 5-3/4% IADB or IBRD loans (as Manufacturers Hanover Trust)
C.A. Venezolana de Desarrollo (Venezuela)	Banco Agrícola y Pecuario (Venezuela)
IFC (Thailand)	Banco Industrial (Peru)
PDC (Philippines)	Nacional Financiera (Mexico)
MIDFL (Malaysia)	Banco Nacional de Costa Rica (Costa Rica)
Industrialization Fund (Finland)	Austrian Investment Credit Corporation (Austria)

4. Morgan Guarantee International Finance Corporation (U.S.)

Equity	Debt
	Early maturities, 5-3/4% IADB loans (as Morgan Guarantee Trust Co.)
BNDE (Morocco)	Banco Agrícola y Pecuario (Venezuela)
MIDFL (Malaysia)	Banco de Guatemala (Guatemala)
BDEE (Spain)	

Table 11, Continued

5. Northwest International Bank (U.S.)

Equity	Debt
C.A. Venezolana de Desarrollo (Venezuela) NIDB (Nigeria) BIDI (Ivory Coast) Industrialization Fund Co. (Finland)	None

6. Chemical International Finance (U.S.)

Equity	Debt
	Early maturities, 5-1/2 - 5-3/4% IADB and IBRD loans (as Chemical Corn Exchange Bank New York Trust Co.)
C.A. Venezolana de Desarrollo (Venezuela) PDC (Philippines) Industrialization Fund Co. (Finland)	Banco Agrícola y Pecuario (Venezuela) Banco de la Nación (Argentina) Corporación Venezolana de Fomento (Venezuela) Austrian Investment Credit Corporation (Austria)

7. Chase International Investment Corporation (U.S.)

Equity	Debt
	Early maturities, 5-3/4% IADB loans (Chase Manhattan Bank)
NIDB (Nigeria) BIDI (Ivory Coast) IMBDI (Iran) IFC (Thailand)	Banco Agrícola y Pecuario (Venezuela) CORFO (Chile) Banco de la Nación (Argentina)

Table 11, Continued

8.   Bank of Tokyo (Japan)

Equity	Debt
NIDB (Nigeria)	None
PICIC (Pakistan)	
IFC (Thailand)	
PDC (Philippines)	
MIDCFL (Malaysia)	

9.   Commonwealth Development Finance Corporation (U.K.)

Equity	Debt
NIDB (Nigeria)	None
PICIC (Pakistan)	
ICICI (India)	
MIDFCL (Malaysia)	

10.   Deutche Bank (Germany)

Equity	Debt
BNDE (Morocco)	None
IMBDI (Iran)	
PDC (Philippines)	
MIDFCL (Malaysia)	
Industrialization Fund Co. (Finland)	
BDEE (Spain)	

Source: Annual reports and press releases of the
          IBRD and IDB.

Table 12

Selected Financial Institutions with Investments
in at Least One Development Bank

Bank	Investment	Bank	Investment
		NEW YORK	
1. First National City Bank (First National City Overseas Investment Corp.)	Debt Equity	6. Continental Bank International, New York	Debt
2. Bankers Trust Co. (Bankers International Financing Co.)	Debt Equity	7. Grace National Bank	Debt
3. Irving Trust Co. (Irving International Financing Corporation)	Debt Equity	8. J. Henry Schroeder Bank Corporation	Debt
4. Manufacturers Hanover Trust (Manufacturers Hanover IFC)	Debt Equity	9. Morgan Guarantee Trust Co. (Morgan Guarantee IFC)	Debt Equity
5. Meadow Brook National Bank	Debt	10. Chemical Corn Exchange Bank New York Trust Co. Chemical Int'l. Finance Co.	Debt Equity
		11. Chase Manhattan Bank (Chase International Investment Corporation)	Equity

12. New York Hanseatic Co. — Equity
13. Development and Resources Co. — Equity
14. International Basic Economy Co. — Debt

15. Bankers Trust Co. — Debt
16. Marine Midland Trust Co. — Debt
17. American Express Co., Inc. — Debt

PENNSYLVANIA

1. Philadelphia National Bank (Philadelphia International Investment Co.) — Debt
2. First Penn. Banking and Trust Co. — Debt

3. Fidelity Philadelphia Trust — Debt
4. Girard Trust Corn Exchange Bank — Equity
5. Mellon National Bank and Trust Co. — Debt

WASHINGTON, D. C.

1. American Security and Trust Co. — Debt

2. National Bank of Washington — Debt

Table 12, Continued

Bank	Investment	Bank	Investment
BOSTON			
1. The Boston Corporation	Equity	3. The National Shawmut Bank	Debt
2. First National Bank, Boston	Debt		
ILLINOIS-OHIO			
1. Continental Illinois National Bank and Trust Co.	Debt	4. (Northwest International Bank)	Equity
2. Central National Bank, Cleveland	Debt	5. First National Bank, Chicago	Debt
3. Harris Trust and Savings Bank, Chicago	Debt	6. Northern Trust Co.	Debt
		7. American National Bank and Trust Co. of Chicago	Debt
CALIFORNIA			
1. United California Bank, L.A.	Debt	4. Crocker Citizens National Bank	Debt
2. Union Bank, Los Angeles	Debt	5. Wells Fargo Bank, San Francisco	Debt
3. Bank of California	Debt		

FRANCE

1. Lazard Freres — Equity
2. Caisse Central de Coopera-tion Economique — Equity
3. Banque Francaise du Commerce Exterior — Equity
4. Credit Lyonnaise — Equity
5. Societe Financiere pour les Pays d'Outre Mer — Equity
6. Caisse de Depots et Consignations — Equity
7. De Rothschild Freres — Equity
8. Banque de Paris et de Pays Bas — Equity

UNITED KINGDOM

1. The Chartered Bank (Hong Kong) — Equity
2. Eastern Exchange Banks(8) — Equity
3. Lloyds Bank, Ltd. — Equity
4. Barclays Bank — Equity
5. Midland Bank — Equity
6. Hong Kong and Shanghai Bank — Equity
7. United Commercial Bank — Equity
8. Colonial Development Co. — Equity
9. Branchman-Wirtz and Co. — Equity
10. Commonwealth Development Finance Co. — Equity

Table 12, Continued

Bank	Investment	Bank	Investment
		UNITED KINGDOM (cont'd)	
11. Commonwealth Development Co.	Equity	13. Lehman Bros.	Equity
		14. Mercantile Bank	Equity
12. C.A. Inversiones Shell de Venezuela	Equity	15. United Commercial Bank	Equity
		GERMANY	
1. Deutche Bank	Equity	4. Commerz Bank A.G.	Debt
2. Dresdner Bank, Hamburg	Debt	5. Westfallen Bank	Equity
3. Oppenheim and Son	Equity	6. Hanbros Bank	Equity
		OTHERS	
Italy			
Istituto Mobiliare Italiano	Equity	Banca Nazionale del Lavoro, Rome	Equity
Monte Catini	Equity	Medio Banca	Equity
		Fiat S.P.A.	Equity

Sweden		
Scandinaviska Banken	Equity	Aktiebolaget Investor	Equity
Japan		
Bank of Tokyo	Equity	Mitsui Bank	Equity
Netherland		
Algemene Bank Nederland	Equity		

Source: IBRD, IDB, IFC Annual Reports and Press Releases.

financial houses in the United States and in Europe known to be interested in these kinds of participations, outlining the terms of the participations and making the offer.

Because of the tremendous paper work involved in notifying the participator that the loan has been signed, confirming the amount of his participation, drawing up and signing a participation agreement and a loan contract, in addition to pari passu disbursement agreements, and notification with respect to borrower repayment, no loan under $5 million is offered for participation. The private banks are usually interested in taking the early maturities on these loans in order to minimize their own risk and in order to make their position maximally liquid.

One of the reasons for the public and international lending agencies seeking participation is that if participations are forthcoming it is a demonstration to the financial community that it has made a bankable loan. It thus gets the private financial community used to the idea of limited exposure of international lending.

From the standpoint of the private financial community, participations can be a lucrative and liquid form of investment although this is probably not the principal reason why it participates. One of the principal reasons seems to be that the private banking community senses that the trend of the future is in investment overseas and it feels, too, that it is gaining valuable experience in dealing with risks of international investment. Another reason which may or may not be important, depending on the particular case, is the fact that the bank may feel an obligation to participate in view of other aspects of its relationship with the public or international body. For example, the public lending agency has to make use of private commercial banks for normal banking functions. Private commercial banks may feel an obligation to participate with the public lending agency because of the fact that the public agency is also a customer. Naturally, the strength of this motive is difficult to assess. Nevertheless it does probably exist.

It is quite likely that participations in the near future at any rate may not be quite as extensive as they have been in the past. There has been a suggestion, in view of the current U.S. balance of payments crisis, that the U.S. banking system limit the increase in its portfolio abroad to 5 per cent of the amount that existed December 31, 1964. Because no commercial bank wants to be in a position to say to a good client that it cannot accommodate his request for private investment overseas, commercial banks are quite likely to restrict their participation in the loans of public and international agencies so as to free their portfolio for such accommodation.

In the future Europe is not likely to be a good source of participation for such loans because rates are not competitive. The 6 per cent charged by the Inter-American Bank and the 5.5 per cent charged by the World Bank on its loans are not competitive with interest rates that can be obtained in Europe. The Inter-American Development Bank regularly solicits 40 European houses for participation and occasionally does obtain European participation although one intuitively feels that such participation is being rendered out of an obligation by the European house to a good client or for some other reason than the inducement of the interest rate. Because of the higher rates in Europe, BID charges an additional 1.5 per cent on money obtained by bond issues in Europe.

As can be seen in Tables 11 and 12, private financial institutions have taken extensive equity positions in development banks abroad. The reasons are probably as follows:

a. They have obtained thus the ability to refer customers to this bank for local advice.

b. They thus obtain a window into the country and are better able to identify and evaluate profit opportunities.

c. They thus obtain a presence in the country and enhance their image.

d. They thus obtain the goodwill of the country by associating themselves with popular development finance institutions.

e. They obtain contacts within the country that may lead to other valuable indirect benefits.

Individual banks have different techniques for attaining the above objectives. The First National City Bank, for example, and the Bank of America establish branch banks in these countries. Other banks affiliate with local banks and still others may take equity positions in development banks.

A commercial bank can take an equity position in a development bank only through its Edge Act corporations, which are corporations set up under the amendment of Senator Edge to the law regulating the activities of commercial banks.

Corporations, cooperatives, other institutions, and even individuals have in the past invested and are likely in the future to invest in development banks either through the purchase of equity shares or through the purchase of debt obligations, for one or more of the following reasons:

a. To improve one's image in the country. This has been found a very valuable technique to many private corporations which have subsidiaries or other interests in a developing country. They enjoy and benefit from being associated with a private development bank.

b. Such an investment can be a source of profit to the investor since although earnings in the beginning are likely to be small, growth potential is great, and the security of a diversified portfolio is also great.

c. The private investor may consider such investment as an entry into that country.

d. Such an investment may also be considered by the investor as a source of information about profit opportunities in that country.

For these and other reasons many people feel that the private foreign source of capital is a major untapped source of funds for development banks both for equity and for debt. It is patently apparent that through investment in a development bank an investor is receiving protection of a diversified portfolio and has a front row opportunity to participate in the tremendous growth that lies ahead for all developing countries.

Conclusion

One can see that capital has been attracted to development banks from many different sources and for many different reasons. It is highly likely that the use of this type of financial institution by these sources as a channel for their capital will increase, at least for the next few years.

In the long run, however, development banking as a special field of banking will cease to exist. The functions now being performed by development banks (term lending, equity investment, underwriting, guaranteeing, technical assistance, and so on) gradually will be undertaken by specialized institutions or by fragments of the same institution.

One of the principal benefits of a development bank is that it continually reminds practitioners of development that finance, unaccompanied by technical assistance and unrelated to development objectives, is likely to be sterile. Again and again we have been reminded that financing, though necessary, is not a sufficient condition of development.

And yet bankers are not born conservative. They are made that way by the pain and heartache of the first bad loan they make. A banker can easily spend more of his valuable time and effort trying to rectify or salvage a loan he has made to a borrower who is in trouble than he will spend in servicing the entire balance of his portfolio.

On the other hand, many intuitively feel that conservativism and development are inherently incompatible because of the risks involved in financing projects in the less developed countries. Some of the more conservative bankers, even when they have the funds to lend, become "gun shy" when called upon to release funds to a borrower in a developing country because of the myriad "unforeseen events" that can cause an otherwise good loan to go sour. Inflation, balance of payments problems, and political upheaval are a few of the unpredictables involved.

Ideally, then, the development banker has to achieve some kind of balance between the cold fish-eye approach of a traditional commercial banker and the enthusiastic drumbeat of the promoter. This balance will depend on many factors relating to the country, the project, and the bank itself.

But the balance must be achieved. Loans and investments must be made for projects which add to the productive capacities of the emerging countries, because the achievements of modern technology have challenged all societies - both primitive and developed - to do a more effective job in channeling scarce resources to satisfy unlimited wants. From an economist's point of view, that's what development is.

Note to Chapter 3

1. Business International, August through October, 1964, issues.

APPENDIX A

Information Required by the
Inter-American Development Bank for the
Evaluation of a Financial Institution

1. ## General

   In order to be able to evaluate a financial institution
   and decide whether or not it is capable of being a subject
   of credit, it is necessary to obtain widely varied and
   complete information about its legal structure, administration, financial structure, operating policies, systems
   of control, and the economic, social, and financial
   results obtained.

2. ## Legal and Administrative Structure ✓

   (a) ## Purpose of Organization

   Text of charter or law authorizing its establishment,
   and the by-laws currently in force

   (b) ## General Information

   Date of establishment
   Date of commencement of operations
   Ownership and control (public, mixed, or private)
   Principal shareholders
   Country or, in the case of a regional organization,
       member countries

   (c) ## Administration

   Membership and method of selecting a board of
       directors and other officials
   Voting power of shareholders
   Description and duties of special committees

    Number and duties of technical staff
    Number and duties of administrative staff
    Number and location of branches and agencies
    Plans for reorganizing the institution

(d) Table of Organization

3.   Financial Structure ✓

   (a) Capital and Reserves

       Authorized capital
       Subscribed and paid-in capital
       Distribution of shares
       Reserves
       Investments
       Financial program

   (b) Means of Obtaining Funds

       Current accounts
       Time deposits
       Savings
       Issue of securities
       Authorization to contract external loans
       Loans obtained - external and internal
       Availability of foreign exchange
       Subsidies and contributions from the state or
          other sources

   (c) The Institution Vis-a-Vis Monetary Policy

       Access to central bank
       Provisions applicable to rediscount operations
       Provisions governing legal reserves

   (d) Status of Portfolio

       Amount and number of outstanding loans
       Distribution by sectors
       Distribution by terms of repayment
       Distribution by guarantees
       Distribution by interest rates
       Percentage of recovery

4.   Operating Policy ✓

   (a) Sphere of Influence

      National
      Special regions
      Underdeveloped areas

   (b) Sphere of Operations

      Intrastructure
      Agriculture
      Industry
      Transportation
      Housing
      Commerce
      Public utilities
      Hotel and tourism

   (c) Eligible Borrowers

      Public
      Private
      Local
      Foreign

   (d) Activities Financed

      Promotion of new enterprises
      Expansion of existing enterprises
      Modernization of enterprises

   (e) Utilization of Financing and Currencies Loaned

      Working capital
      Refinancing
      Local currency
      Assumption of exchange risk
      Maintenance of value of currencies loaned
      Use of foreign exchange to finance local costs

   (f) Ineligible or Restricted Projects

      Description by objectives (radio, television, alco-
      holic beverage, factory, luxury items for local

consumption, newspaper companies, etc.)

5. Basic Loan Criteria √

(a) General Consideration

Priorities for country development
Economic benefits
Social considerations
Portfolio considerations
Scale of limits on loans
Maximum and minimum amounts
Ratio of loan to net worth
Percentage of participation required by borrower

(b) Guarantee of Loans

Mortgages
Chattel mortgages
Bank guarantees
Negative pledge clauses (prohibiting the borrower
from incurring new obligations)

(c) Maturities on Loans

(d) Interest Rates

(e) Service Charges

(f) Prepayment Provision

(g) Restrictions Imposed on Borrowers

Limitation on dividends
Compensation for directors
Limitations on sale of outstanding shares and on the
issue of new shares
Limitations on the encumbrance of assets
Minimum insurance
Participation in management

(g) Flow Chart of Operations

6. Coordination, Promotion, and Integration Activities √

(a) Economic Planning Functions

Economic studies
Relationship to economic or social programs of the
government

(b) Coordination

Coordination with other private or public development institutions
Is borrower required to exhaust all possibilities of
financing from private sources?

(c) Role in Encouragement of Capital Markets

Promotional campaign
Training courses
Activities in securities market

(d) Technical Assistance

Technical supervision of loans
Assistance in accounting and auditing procedures
Assistance to borrowers in preparing applications

(e) Latin American Economic Integration

Relationship of programs to Latin American
economic integration

7. Procedures and Control

(a) Provisions Usually Included in Loan Contracts

Supervision of loans

(b) Audit

External
Internal
Appointment of auditor

(c) Procurement Policy

Competitive bidding as opposed to negotiated contracts

Policy concerning purchases of domestic goods
Policy concerning purchases of imported goods

8. Results Obtained

(a) In this section, there should be outlined the economic social and financial results obtained since the establishment of the institution.

9. Other Information

The data listed in the preceding paragraphs make it possible to arrive at conclusions on the institutional capacity of the development bank, but it is necessary to have additional information on the program of investments for loans which it is proposed to make with IDB funds. The basic description of the investment plan for the proposed activity must include the following details:

(a) Kind

Total amount of credit and repayment plan

(b) Possible Demand for Sub-loans Indicating the Basis for the Estimate

(c) Availability of Necessary Agencies and Other Services for the Implementation of the Plan

(d) Proposed Administration of the Plan

For the sake of achieving uniformity in the presentation of investment plans, the IDB will supply upon request proforma models of investment plans.

APPENDIX B

Export-Import Bank
Information Required of Prospective Borrowers

1. Describe the materials, equipment, and services involved, the estimated cost thereof, and the amount of financial assistance sought from the Export-Import Bank.

2. Describe the use which will be made of the goods and services in the country of import.

3. Indicate the repayment schedule and other credit terms desired.

4. Show that the assistance necessary to finance the transaction is not available from sources other than the Export-Import Bank.

5. For private borrowers only:

   (a) Describe the project for which United States materials and equipment and associated services are desired and indicate whether it is likely to lead to new industries or expansion of existing ones.

   (b) Present engineering data and market surveys as appropriate to the extent that they are available for possible sub-loans.

   (c) Indicate the extent to which prospective U.S. suppliers might participate in the financing if such information is available at the time the development bank is applying for the loan.

   (d) Give separately the estimated dollar expenditures for the project and the estimated expenditures in local and other currencies.

(e) Show what portion of the total capital will be pro-
     vided for the project in the form of equity and what
     forms of investment including the loan requested
     would provide the remainder of the total capital
     required.

(f) If the project is the expansion of an existing industry,
     include as many financial details on the firm as pos-
     sible including balance sheets, profit and loss state-
     ments for the last three to five years and for all
     projects estimated forecasted balance sheets and
     profit and loss statements for three years after
     completion of the project.

(g) Indicate whether a guarantee of repayment of the
     proposed loan could be offered and, if so, by whom.

(h) Where exchange controls are in effect, indicate
     whether the Export-Import Bank could be furnished
     an assurance by the proper authority of the country
     of import that United States dollars will be made
     available upon payment of local currency to meet
     payments of interest and principal to the bank as
     they fall due.

6. If the borrower is a government or a political subdivision
    the following information is solicited:

(a) Describe the project for which United States mate-
     rials, equipment, and associated services are
     desired.

(b) Present engineering and economic data and market
     surveys to the extent that they are pertinent and
     available.

(c) Indicate whether the project will be self-liquidating
     or whether repayment will be paid from other
     revenues.

(d) Show the total amount of funds required for the pro-
     ject and show the amounts and sources of funds other
     than those requested from the bank.

(e) Give separately the estimated dollar expenditures

for the project and the estimated expenditures in local and other currencies.

(f) State the external assets of the country in the form of gold and foreign exchange showing official holdings separate from private holdings and holdings of dollars and other convertible currencies separate from the holdings of inconvertible currencies.

(g) State the international investment position of the country at short term and long term including major commitments pending or contemplated and an estimate of the amount of interest and amortization due in dollars and other convertible currencies on all external fixed service obligations as well as on commercial accounts, if any, annually over the life of the loan.

(h) Give the current and prospective balance of payments of the country.

(i) If the application is on behalf of a public entity other than the national government, state the financial and legal relationship of the entity to that government and show whether a payment by the entity would be guaranteed by that government or its central bank.

Source: Export-Import Bank Office of Public Information

APPENDIX C

Information Required by AID
for Consideration of a
Loan to a Development Bank

This outline covers information required for an application from an existing bank. When application is made by sponsors of a proposed new bank, information should be supplied to the extent that it is available. All information, including required documents, must be supplied in the English language.

1. The Applicant

   (a) Official name of the institution
   (b) Mail and cable addresses
   (c) Nature of present operations (types of loans made, purpose, terms, etc., with references to applicable provisions in charter, by-laws, and policy statements)
   (d) Legal basis of the institution, including any statutory authority, articles of agreement or charter, and other founding documents
   (e) Any general policy statements covering operations of the bank
   (f) Geographic area of operations

2. Names and Brief Biographic Sketches of Founders

   (a) Capitalization, equity and debt, how raised, subscribers, including brief biographic sketches, terms of debt capital, etc.
   (b) Balance sheets and profit and loss statements covering each of the previous five years of operations
   (c) Description of organization structure of the bank
   (d) Brief biographic sketches of the directors of the

174

bank, including present full-time positions and
any information indicating financial experience
(e) Management - full biographic sketches indicating
qualifications and principal previous employ-
ments
(f) Professional and technical staff--full biographic
descriptions of principal staff members and
brief biographic sketches of remainder of staff,
indicating professional qualifications and experience.
(g) Brief description of procedures of the bank

3. Current Agricultural and/or Industrial Credit Needs
in the Applicant's Country

(a) The importance of agriculture and/or industry
in applicant's country

(1) Statistics re agricultural undertakings,
industrial establishments, capital investment, value of production, small industrial development, etc.
(2) Relationship of agriculture and/or industry to growth of economy
(3) Prospective agricultural and/or industrial
development required to serve domestic
market; export possibilities
(4) General climate for agricultural and/or
industrial development

(b) Agricultural and/or industrial credit needs

(1) Investment over the past decade
(2) Estimates in agriculture in next ten years
(3) Other development banks in the country
(4) Other commercial banks - scope of their
operations

4. AID Loan Request

(a) Amount of loan requested with a justification
for this amount. The justification should include
the time period in which the bank expects the
funds to be lent and some basis for this
estimate.

(b) Proposed use of funds. This should include a description of the type of loans to be made, maturities of the loans, the amount of equity which will be required from borrowers of the bank, the amount and kind of security which will be required from borrowers, the interest rate which will normally be charged and a form copy of the loan agreement which will normally be used.

(c) Repayment schedules which will be requested from AID

(d) Proposed interest rate and justification thereof

(e) The nature of the government guarantee, if applicable

(f) Description of how the bank intends to apply funds available to it, including both local and foreign currencies

5. <u>Estimated General Results of the Proposed Loan</u>

(a) Kind and amount of agricultural and/or industrial and other development it would make possible

(b) Benefits accruing to the applicant's national economy as a result of (a) above

(c) Relation to over-all development program of applicant's country

(d) Effect, if any, on the foreign exchange position of the applicant's country

(e) Other material which would serve as justification arguments, such as:

(1) Whether financing can be obtained in whole or in part from other Free World sources on reasonable terms

(2) The consistency of the activity with, and its relation to, other development activities being undertaken or planned and its potential contribution to the realization of the long-range activities

(3) The extent to which the recipient country is being responsive to the economic, political and social needs of its people and a demonstration of the country's determination to take effective self-help measures

(4) The possible effects of the loan on the

United States economy with special reference to areas of substantial labor surplus, and also its effect on United States balance of payments

6. Operations Projection

Pro forma operating statements covering the first five years of operations following the AID loan showing interest charges, interest payments, operating expenses, etc., including net profit for each year and the proposed distribution thereof.

7. Other

Applicant should describe attempts made to obtain credit from either public, international, or private lending institutions, stocks subscriptions, etc. Also the applicant should describe the role which any foreign government or international institution, such as IBRD, has played in the establishment and/or the operation of the bank.

Source: AID Policy Guideline No. 2, March 12, 1962.

ABOUT THE AUTHOR

J. T. Dock Houk has had wide experience in development banking. He is presently Assistant Director of the Inter-American Cooperative Bank Development Program, which is helping to establish a loan program for Latin American cooperatives. Mr. Houk was a member of the Near East South Asia Capital Development Division of the Agency for International Development. He is on the faculty of the University of Virginia and has taught development banking at American University in Washington, D. C.

Mr. Houk's education included study in economics and law at Brown University, Svenska Handelshogskolan in Helsinki, and LaSalle University. He received his Ph. D. degree from American University.

Date Due